Sheila Gordon
Lady Anne's Way

Illustrations by Frank Gordon

Published by Skyware Ltd.

Published in 2025 by
Skyware Ltd.
48 Albert Avenue
Saltaire
Shipley BD18 4NT
www.skyware.co.uk

ISBN 978 1 911321 08 8

First published by Skyware Ltd. 2013, 2019.
Originally published by Hillside Publications 1995, 2003.

Text © Sheila Gordon 2025
Illustrations © Frank Gordon 2025
Route maps © Tony Grogan 2025

All rights reserved. No part of this book may be reproduced in any form or by any means without permission in writing from the publisher.

Main route maps based on current OS Explorer maps 1:25,000 series. Reproduced by permission of Ordnance Survey on behalf of HMSO. © Crown copyright 2025. All rights reserved. Ordnance Survey Licence number AC0000820417. Other maps based on OS Opendata. Contains Ordnance Survey data © Crown copyright and database right 2025.

British Library Cataloguing-in-Publication Data.
A catalogue record for this book is available from the British Library.

Every care has been taken in the preparation of this book and all the information has been carefully checked and is believed to be correct at the time of publication. However, the countryside changes and neither the author nor the publishers can accept responsibility for any errors or omissions or for any loss, damage, injury or inconvenience resulting from the use of this book.

Printed by Hart & Clough Ltd., Ezra House, West 26 Business Park, Cleckheaton BD19 4TQ

Dedicated to a great northern lady

The Great Picture (triptych). *Left panel*: Lady Anne Clifford aged 15, when she was disinherited. *Centre Panel*: Lady Anne's parents - Margaret Russell and George Clifford, third Earl of Cumberland, with her older brothers who did not survive to adulthood: Francis and Robert. *Right panel*: Lady Anne aged 56, when she reclaimed her inheritance.

Reproduced by courtesy of the Abbot Hall Art Gallery, Lakeland Arts Trust, Kendal, Cumbria.

FOREWORD

For almost thirty years, Lady Anne Clifford was virtually a queen in the dale-country of Craven and Westmorland. Lady Anne liked to visit her five Castles and Barden Tower in turn. Lady Anne's Way, as selected by the author, covers a hundred miles through quiet dales and across heather moors. It is vividly described in this book which, from the point of view of its author, combines her love of walking with a love of local history. Stride along the grassy Stake Pass from Wharfedale to Wensleydale. Stand in the ruins of Pendragon Castle, in romantic Mallerstang. Admire Lady Anne's tomb in a fine old church at Appleby. Then complete the journey by the River Eden to historic Brougham.

W R Mitchell, MBE

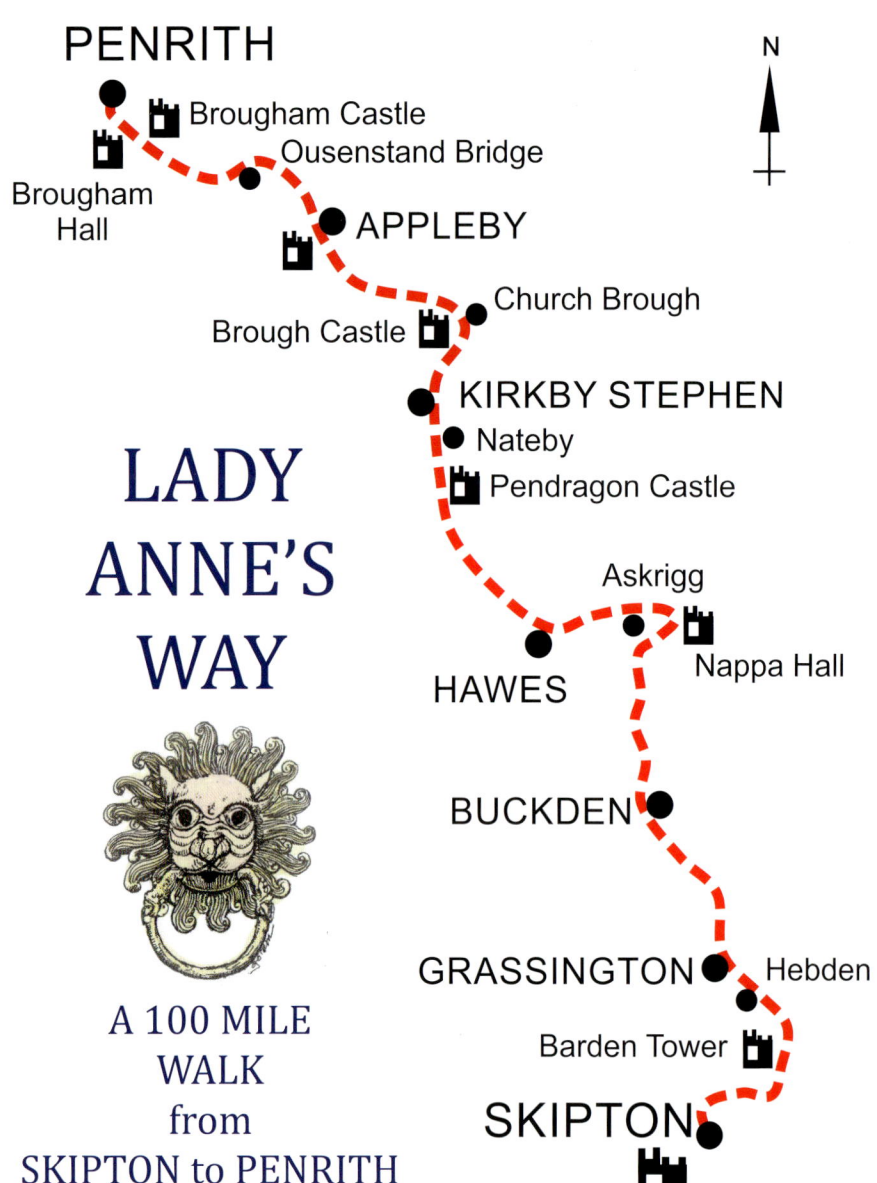

THE STAGES
- including stage and cumulative mileages

STAGE 1: SKIPTON to GRASSINGTON
- 15½ miles (25.1 km)   [*15½ miles (25.1 km)*]

STAGE 2: GRASSINGTON to BUCKDEN
- 12½ miles (20.2 km)   [*28 miles (45.3 km)*]

STAGE 3: BUCKDEN to HAWES
- 18 miles (28.9 km)   [*46 miles (74.2 km)*]

STAGE 4: HAWES to KIRKBY STEPHEN
- 17¼ miles (27.8 km)   [*63¼ miles (102.0 km)*]

STAGE 5: KIRKBY STEPHEN to APPLEBY
- 16½ miles (26.6 km)   [*79¾ miles (128.6 km)*]

STAGE 6: APPLEBY to PENRITH
- 19¾ miles (31.9 km)   [*99½ miles (160.5 km)*]

---

9 - Day version

1: **SKIPTON to HEBDEN** - 13¾ miles (22.1 km)

2: **HEBDEN to BUCKDEN** - 14¼ miles (22.9 km)

3: **BUCKDEN to ASKRIGG** - 12¼ miles (19.7 km)

4: **ASKRIGG to HAWES** - 5¾ miles (9.3 km)

5: **HAWES to NATEBY** - 15½ miles (24.9 km)

6: **NATEBY to CHURCH BROUGH** - 8 miles (12.9 km)

7: **CHURCH BROUGH to APPLEBY** - 10¼ miles (16.5 km)

8: **APPLEBY to OUSENSTAND BRIDGE** - 8¼ miles (13.3 km)

9: **OUSENSTAND BRIDGE to PENRITH** - 11½ miles (18.5 km)

Contents

Forward by Bill Mitchell 3
Overview map 4
The Stages 5
Contents 6
Introduction 7
Route finding...**9**; Equipment...**9**; Route stages...**10**; Getting there...**11**.
Stage One: SKIPTON TO GRASSINGTON **12**
*Skipton to Bark Lane...**14**; Bark Lane to Barden Bridge...**17**; Barden Bridge to Burnsall...**19**; Burnsall to Grassington...**21**;*
Stage Two: GRASSINGTON TO BUCKDEN **24**
*Grassington to Bycliffe Rd...**25**; Bycliffe Rd. to Kettlewell...**27**; Kettlewell to Birks Wood...**30**; Buckden...**31**; Birks Wood to Hell Gap...**32**.*
Stage Three: BUCKDEN TO HAWES **33**
*Hell Gap to Busk Lane...**34**; Busk Lane to Worton...**36**; Worton to Skell Gill...**38**; Skell Gill to Hawes...**42**; Hawes...**43**.*
Stage Four: HAWES TO KIRKBY STEPHEN **44**
*Hawes to Cotter Riggs...**45**; Cotter Riggs to High Dyke...**47**; High Dyke to Old Road...**49**; Old Road to Pendragon...**53**; Pendragon...**54**; Pendragon to Nateby...**55**; Kirkby Stephen...**56**; Nateby to Winton...**58**.*
Stage Five: KIRKBY STEPHEN TO APPLEBY **59**
*Winton to Church Brough...**61**; Brough...**63**; Church Brough to Warcop...**64**; Warcop to Little Ormside...**67**; Little Ormside to Appleby...**71**.*
Stage Six: APPLEBY TO PENRITH **75**
*Appleby to Long Marton...**76**; Long Marton to Ousenstand Bridge...**79**; Temple Sowerby alternative by road...**80**; Temple Sowerby option by footpath...**82**; Ousenstand Bridge to Cliburn...**83**; Cliburn to Clifton Dykes...**87**; Clifton Dykes to Penrith...**88**.*
Select bibliography **94**
Acknowledgements **95**
Key to strip maps **95**

(Opposite) Summer hay meadows in Mallerstang, with Wild Boar Fell beyond.

INTRODUCTION

The inspiration for Lady Anne's Way came to me whilst attending a lecture on 'The River Ure and its Source', when a reference was made to Lady Anne's Highway in Mallerstang. On hearing that this great lady owned many impressive and historic castles scattered all over Northern England, I was immediately struck with the idea of a long distance path that would not only link these beautiful buildings but would also be my own tribute to a remarkable woman. A close scrutiny of the relevant Ordnance Survey maps showed that a walk of approximately one hundred miles could quite happily be worked out, and so the route was born.

Lady Anne Clifford was the last in the line of that great family the Cliffords, who owned vast estates extending from Skipton in Craven to Brougham in Westmorland. Much of the land included wild and rugged country at the head of Wharfedale and Wensleydale, as well as Mallerstang in the Upper Eden.

Lady Anne was born in 1590 in Skipton Castle and was the only surviving child of George Clifford, 3rd Earl of Cumberland, and his wife Margaret Russell. On her father's death in 1605 she failed to inherit the estate which passed instead to her uncle and his male heirs. This injustice was felt very deeply by both Lady Anne and her mother and in future years was to be a bone of contention between Lady Anne and her husbands. It marked a turning point in her life and, greatly encouraged and assisted by her mother, she spent the next thirty eight years trying to regain her inheritance.

She was married twice. Firstly to Richard Sackville, Earl of Dorset who died in 1624; and then six years later to Philip Herbert, Earl of Pembroke and Montgomery. This second marriage was not a happy one and after four and a half years they quarrelled and subsequently lived apart. The Earl of Pembroke died in 1650. Prior to this in 1649 Lady Anne left the South of England forever. It had been her home since childhood but in 1643 she had at last come into her rightful inheritance and now was the time to return to the land of her birth and set her houses in order.

Her estates and, more particularly, her castles were in great need of repair and the restoration of these was to be her self-imposed task for the rest of her life. She was sixty years old when she started this project, restoring not only her castles but also nearby churches. She also built almshouses for the needy. Lady Anne was strict with her tenants but always very fair in any disputes; she could be very generous to those who worked for her and gave frequently to the poor. Whilst supervising the work on her castles she would travel to each one in turn, sometimes spending months at a time at each. She spent a lot of time at Appleby but Brougham remained her favourite, and was to be the castle in which she eventually died.

In devising this walk my aim has been to follow in spirit some of the routes taken by Lady Anne, whilst visiting all her important buildings on the way. I wished to strike a balance between sticking religiously to her routes (a great deal of which now lie under tarmac, making them intolerable to walk on for more than brief stretches) while gaining a true flavour of the surrounding landscape. I had no desire to increase the pressure on existing long distance paths, nor to stay totally in the valleys, beautiful though they are, and so I have taken to the fellsides whenever possible.

I discovered that minor duplication of routes was inevitable on some stages, most notably the section of the Dales Way in Wharfedale from Barden to Burnsall. However, because Barden Tower was such an important building to the Clifford family, and as no continuous footpath exists on the other side of the river, I felt justified in using it.

The most well known section of the walk is the route out of Wensleydale, up Cotter End and along Mallerstang which is still known today as The Highway. Here perhaps more than anywhere else, it is possible to get a true feeling of how difficult her journey must have been. The land here is wild and rugged and the track exceedingly rough in places. It is supposed that her journeys were made in the drier months of the year and were often broken by an overnight stay at the houses of friends. This would have been a major event for the person extending the hospitality as Lady Anne did not travel light. She herself went in a horse litter, her ladies-in-waiting would be in her coach drawn by six horses; menservants would be on horse-back while many others had to travel on foot. Items of furniture, bedding, tapestries and even a window were taken from castle to castle, ready for a long stay. Often neighbours and friends were press-ganged into accompanying her and the entourage could be as large as three hundred strong on occasions.

On arrival at her destination, the majority were thanked for their endeavours personally and then sent back home. As a thank-you to her hosts, Lady Anne often presented them with a door-lock, made by

Brougham Castle

Walkers pass High Hall on The Highway, Mallerstang

George Dent of Appleby and costing in those days £1. One of these used to be in existence at Dalemain, the home of the Hassell family and situated just north of Ullswater in Cumbria; sadly only the key now remains and is housed in a glass case in the entrance hall. However another can be found at Browsholme Hall, home to the Parker family and situated in Bowland. This is the actual lock with AP proudly carved on it.

The walk is one of great beauty and historical interest; I have organised the book so that the main emphasis is on the route, keeping the history of Lady Anne and her times in the background so that it does not become intrusive. Lady Anne's Way passes through the wonders of the Yorkshire Dales with its unspoilt villages and its limestone pavements and progresses through the remote and rugged fellside of Mallerstang, to enter Cumbria and the romantic delights and hidden haunts of the Eden Valley. This is a walk for anyone who is reasonably fit, with a sense of adventure and a love of our countryside; it will appeal both to seasoned walkers and those seeking their first experience of a long distance path.

ROUTE FINDING

The route is waymarked throughout and the detailed strip maps in the book, together with the text, should make route finding straight forward but I would always recommend carrying the relevant Ordnance Survey maps and a compass. I apologise in advance for any inaccuracies which may occur in the route description; this was correct when going to press but after the passage of time, gates and stiles are altered, walls and fences are removed and the structure and colour of buildings changed.

EQUIPMENT

Wet weather gear is always essential in our green and pleasant land, even on the sunniest of days, particularly as some of the sections of the walk are quite remote. Good footwear is another important and controversial issue. In recent years lightweight boots and track shoes have become the norm in certain sections of the walking movement, being favoured over the heavy, traditional boot normally associated with long-distance walking. The choice is yours; the important point is that your footwear should be comfortable and hard-wearing and give you confidence. For myself I have gone through a period of wearing lightweights without any problems but have returned to slightly heavier boots with ankle support after suffering a broken ankle.

Always carry some emergency food, a First Aid kit and water. The latter can be most important on a hot day high in the fells, where the nearest water supply can be many miles away. It goes without saying that map and compass should always be with you and that you must know how to use them. I don't wish to pontificate on the entire contents of your rucksack as, if you are a regular walker, you will have this information anyway. All I will say further on the point is BE PREPARED.

There are now several carriers who will take your gear onto the next stage for you. Accommodation can be booked through them and itineraries tailored to your needs. A search of the web will reveal all.

River Wharfe near Appletreewick

ROUTE STAGES

The route divides naturally into 6 stages, each finishing at a town or village where accommodation is available. Seasoned walkers might tackle one stage each day however most people will find some sections too long. It is better to break them and take time to explore. If you prefer the walk can be covered in 9 days (see page 5 for suggested itinerary).

Accommodation and facilities will be harder to find however in the smaller villages and hamlets. There are no facilities at Ousenstand Bridge, however accommodation can be found just over a mile off route at Temple Sowerby. A more detailed description of this fascinating village can be found in the relevant section.

Appleby boasts lots of amenities but be forewarned that bed and breakfast accommodation could be a problem at the beginning of June, when there is none to be had for miles in and around the town. During this period the horse-fair is in progress and accommodation tends to be booked well in advance.

Hostels are situated at Kettlewell, Hawes,

Brougham Hall

Kirkby Stephen and Dufton, just beyond Appleby. For backpackers the campsite closest to Hebden is at Appletreewick and Kettlewell, Starbotton, Buckden, Askrigg, Hawes, Kirkby Stephen, Appleby, Kirkby Thore and Penrith all have sites. However, if you're not too fastidious about facilities, I have found that an enquiry at the local pub will often produce the name of a farmer willing to let you camp in a field or better still the pub garden.

With the advent of the web it is now far easier to check out accommodation, the availability of village shops and places for an evening meal and the answer is always to plan ahead and ensure you are well stocked. All references to facilities in the text are correct at the time of writing, but please check the website at *www.ladyannesway.co.uk* for useful links and also for any route updates.

GETTING THERE

By far the best means of reaching the route is by rail. Skipton stands on the well served Airedale line from Leeds, which then continues as the Settle-Carlisle line, through the Dales and the Eden Valley to Appleby and Carlisle. Penrith also has a station, on the main line between Lancaster and Carlisle, but is also only 5 miles from Langwathby on the Settle-Carlisle line.

There is a great deal of beautiful countryside out there, go out and enjoy it, but please remember that we must keep it that way for those who come after us. Follow the Country Code and you will have made your contribution to the future preservation of this land of ours:

Enjoy the Countryside and respect its life and work.

Guard against all risk of fire.

Fasten all gates.

Keep dogs under proper control.

Keep to public paths across farm land.

Use gates and stiles to cross fences, hedges and walls.

Leave livestock, crops and machinery alone.

Take your litter home.

Help to keep all water clean.

Protect wildlife, plants and trees.

Take special care on country roads.

Make no unnecessary noise.

If you take only photographs and leave only footprints, you and those coming after you will be welcome.

Happy walking!

Leaving Skipton towards Embsay Moor

STAGE ONE: Skipton to Grassington

Distance: 15½ miles   *Total distance: 15½ miles*

Ordnance Survey Maps 1:25,000 -
Explorer OL 2 – Yorkshire Dales South & West

Stage One takes you through the villages of Embsay and Eastby before going over Halton Edge to reach Barden Tower with its historical associations. Here you will meet the majestic River Wharfe and will follow its banks, visiting many picturesque villages along the way. As you progress through Wharfedale you will notice the field barns and the dry stone walls which are both important features in the Dales landscape. The day ends in the attractive village of Grassington, with its cobbled streets and interesting alleyways. The walking is easy and the scenery is delightful.

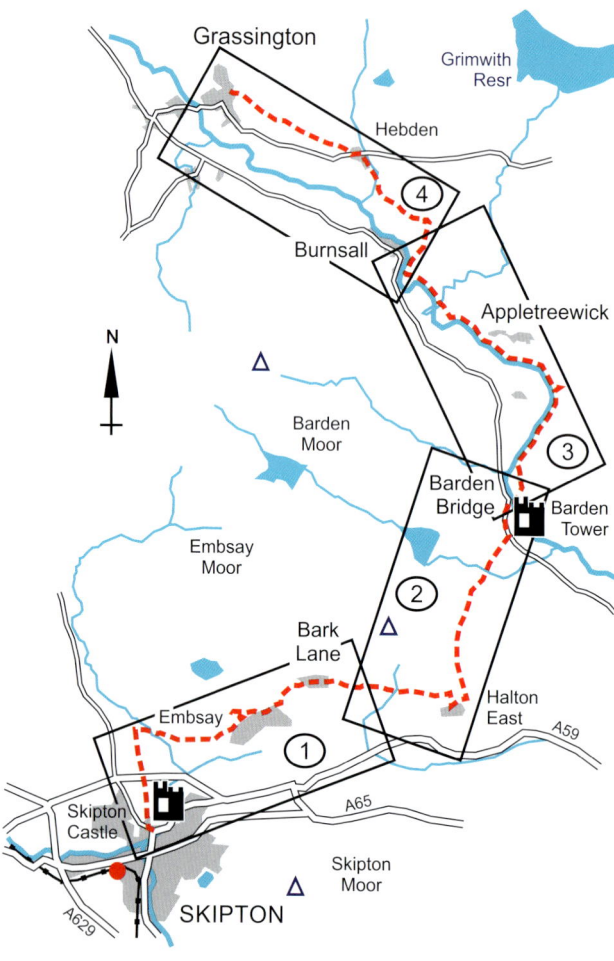

Skipton is well known as the gateway to the Yorkshire Dales. It is a large market town with every amenity and lots to interest the visitor. There are cobbled streets and alleyways to explore, a thriving market four times a week and narrow boats to discover on the Leeds-Liverpool Canal. The town is dominated by Skipton Castle, one of the best preserved medieval castles in England and the birthplace of Lady Anne Clifford, thus making it an ideal starting point for our walk.

The castle stands in a commanding position at the top of the High Street, and was home to the Cliffords from 1310 when it was rebuilt and made stronger by the first Clifford, Lord of Skipton. During the Civil War it withstood a three year siege, and in fact was the only Royalist stronghold remaining in the North of England after the Battle of Marston Moor in July 1644. However, in 1649 it was 'slighted' by Cromwell's men and it was left to Lady Anne in 1657 to start renovation of this remarkable castle. On completion of the work, Lady Anne added a parapet with the Clifford motto DESORMAIS / HENCEFORTH over the main gate, and recorded the work of the restoration on a tablet over the Tudor entrance:

Skipton Castle

THIS SKIPTON CASTLE WAS REPAYRED BY THE LADY ANNE CLIFFORD, COVNTESSE DOWAGER OF PEMBROOKEE, DORSETT, AND MONTGOMERY, BARONESSE CLIFFORD, WESTMERLAND, AND VESEIE, LADY OF THE HONOR OF SKIPTON IN CRAVEN, AND HIGH SHERIFFESSE BY INHERITANCE OF THE COVNTIE OF WESTMORLAND, IN THE YEARES 1657 AND 1658, AFTER THIS MAINE PART OF ITT HAD LAYNE RVINOVS EVER SINCE DECEMBER 1648, AND THE JANVARY FOLLOWINGE, WHEN ITT WAS THEN PVLLD DOWNE AND DEMOLISHT, ALLMOST TO THE FOVNDACON, BY THE COMMAND OF THE PARLIAMENT, THEN SITTING ATT WESTMINSTER, BECAVSE ITT HAD BIN A GARRISON IN THE THEN CIVILL WARRES IN ENGLAND.

ISA. CHAP.58, VER. 12. GODS NAME BE PRAISED..

A year later, to celebrate the restoration work, Lady Anne planted the now famous yew tree in the Conduit Court and this living monument can still be seen to this day.

Adjacent to the castle lies Skipton parish church which she restored in 1655 and where many of her ancestors are buried. A vault was built under the sanctuary in 1542, and this was subsequently enlarged; it contains the bodies of five Earls of Cumberland, three of their Countesses and four of their children. There are two impressive Clifford tombs either side of the High Altar, which are topped with polished black marble slabs and decorated with armorial shields. Burial inside the church was still popular in the early 1800's, but by the middle of the century the smell had become unbearable and the nave floor had to be covered with between 9" and 12" of concrete to seal up all the numerous vaults. Lady Anne herself was buried at the

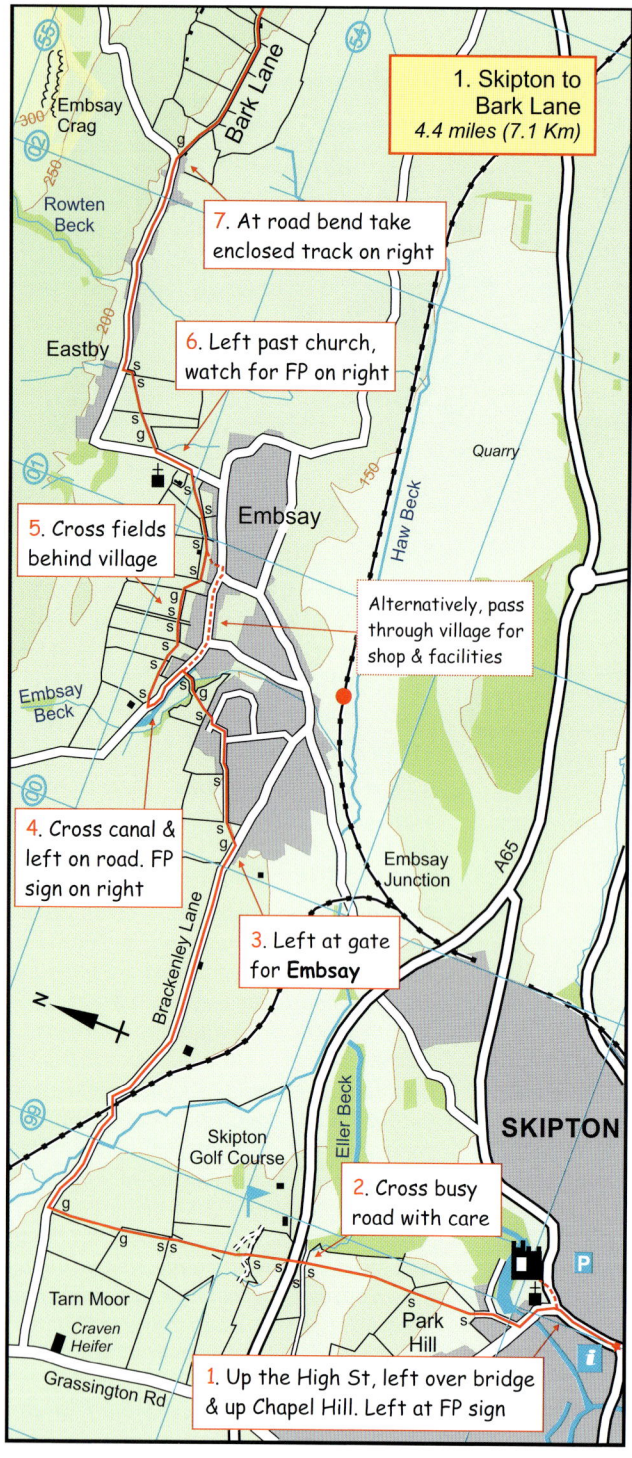

Church of St. Lawrence at Appleby, high in the Eden Valley close to her dear mother.

Both church and castle are well worth a visit, but we must leave the bustle of Skipton and start our journey, following in the footsteps (or should it be carriage tracks?) of that great lady. Visiting her magnificent castles along the way, we can marvel at her strength and determination in tackling such a large renovation project at the age of 60 - a time when most people might be thinking of taking life easy. We start our journey at her birthplace of Skipton and travel through the Yorkshire Dales to reach Mallerstang and the upper Eden Valley in Cumbria, finishing at Brougham Castle on the outskirts of Penrith. Here Lady Anne died in 1676 at the age of 86.

Lady Anne's Way leaves Skipton High Street to the left of the parish church on the B6265 (GR 990519). After crossing the bridge take the first road on your right (Chapel Hill) and a few yards up the hill take the left hand fork (footpath sign here), ignoring the road straight ahead marked 'Private Road No Cars'.

Carry on uphill to a stone stile which leads into a field, climb uphill with a hedge over to your right to reach another stone stile to the left of a gate.

A glance back will show Skipton laid out beneath you, with the tip of the parish church just visible but with the castle hidden amongst the trees. Your route lies in the same general direction as before, across the next field towards Skipton Golf Course, crossing over a stile and a track to reach the Skipton bypass - CROSS WITH GREAT CARE.

Waymarks point the way up the next field and onto the golf course - beware of low flying balls! It's as well to be aware of at least one piece of golfing etiquette here: stand still when golfers are playing a stroke, moving across the fairway only when you are sure the way is clear. Your courtesy will be appreciated. Follow the well waymarked route across the course to reach a wall corner. Follow the wall on your right to go through a squeeze stile followed by another stile. Cross the next field, keeping a fence on your right to reach a gate. Once through here drop down through this field to reach a gate in the bottom left-hand corner which takes you out onto Brackenley Lane (GR 987536).

Turn right and follow this quiet lane for approximately three quarters of a mile to Embsay, passing under a railway bridge. Soon a quarry comes into view, making a dominant feature in the landscape as it eats its way through the hillside. As you approach the village of Embsay, a path appears on the left beyond the 30mph sign and marked Embsay. Follow the path diagonally across the corner of the field to reach a path behind a row of houses which leads into Hill Top Close. Go straight ahead and follow the Close around to the left to reach a T-junction. Cross the road here and take the path to the right of house no. 40, which gives you access to a field. Cross the field and take the path down to Embsay Beck and up onto the road.

The ponds and canal here will have been used to service the mill and are home to many ducks, making a pleasant picture. A left turn here takes you past a delightful seventeenth century building with a sundial above the lintel. After 125 yards take the stone steps on your right up into a field where you need to bear right towards a wall corner. The route is waymarked through a series of fields in an easterly direction to

Embsay

reach Embsay car park (GR 009538). Those needing refreshments or provisions may wish to drop down the field a few yards to reach the village. Embsay is famous for its steam railway which attracts many visitors throughout the year.

Otherwise carry straight on along an obvious path, once again behind houses until you enter a field with a church over to your left amongst the trees. Cross the field diagonally left to reach a gate at the far side at the junction of two walls. Turn left onto Kirk Lane, past the church and across the road to take the paved trod on your right which cuts out a stretch of road walking through Embsay Kirk. The Kirk was originally the site of a priory built by Augustinian monks prior to their settling at Bolton Abbey in the twelfth century. Follow the trod out onto the road, where a right turn will take you after approximately a third of a mile to the old village jail on your left. This building now houses only livestock; it was never used for criminals as such, but merely as an overnight stay for anyone who'd had 'one too many' at the pub which used to be opposite. Follow the road to the end of the village and as the road curves left and starts to climb towards Eastby Crag, take the track on your right known as Bark Lane.

Follow the walled lane to its end and then keep on the track passing through two large fields on your left, until the track peters out. At this point take the stile to the right. Keeping the wall on your left, carry on until you reach a gateway at the end of the stone wall. From here take a diagonal line right, downhill to a stile and stream at the bottom of the incline known as Mawking Hole (GR 032542). Follow the path alongside the wall on the left through three fields. In the fourth one, keep straight on with a fence on your left, to reach a gate ahead. Carry on across the next field to a stile by a gate. Once over this go diagonally right, with a fence on your left, which is waymarked, to reach a group of farm buildings This brings you out onto a farm track. Turn left here to reach a lane. This is Moor Lane and was most probably the one used by Lady Anne on her way from Halton over to Barden Tower. Although it looks very inviting, it is unfortunately not suitable for our purposes and so we must turn right here to reach the T-junction at Halton East. A left turn here takes you past Halton Church Mission Room. Walk up the road for a quarter of a mile and take the path on your left signposted to 'Broad Park' (GR 044542).

You are now crossing the boundary into the Yorkshire Dales National Park, which you will not leave until you reach Nateby at the foot of Mallerstang, about 57 miles away. Follow the line of the wall on your left, past a copse of trees to reach a stile in the wall ahead. In the next field climb uphill diagonally right to a stile in the far right-hand corner of the field. Keep the wall on your right to the next stile and continue along the wall side until the top of Halton Edge is reached. There are superb views from here of Barden Moor over to the left and ahead is your first sight of Wharfedale, with its mixture of high remote fells and idyllic riverside pastures. Its fascinating industrial past and the delightful villages of the present are all ahead waiting to be discovered, and only a short distance away is our next major link with Lady Anne at Barden Tower.

Where the wall swings away to the right, keep straight ahead to reach a green track; turn right on the track for about 10 yards and take the narrow path on your left; if you pass a gate on your right-hand side you've gone too far. The path takes you down the hillside to reach the Barden Road (GR 045559). Ignore the gate out onto the road and turn right along the wall side to reach a gate at the far end of the field which joins the road further along. Turn right along the road for three quarters of a mile, where a left turn at the T-junction brings you onto the B6160 and so to Barden Tower.

This imposing ruin was once home to the 'Shepherd' Lord Clifford in Tudor times, and later to Lady Anne. Although not strictly belonging to her (it had been separated from the Clifford estates at the beginning of the seventeenth century) she took possession of it and stayed in it frequently throughout her life. She was particularly proud of the work she had done to the tower, and whenever any of her relations were staying with her at Skipton Castle they were expected to go over and admire the work.

It was Lady Anne's custom to leave her mark on the buildings which she restored; in the case of Barden Tower, this takes the form of a stone plaque which can be seen on the south wall, and which gives details of the renovation work:

THIS BARDEN
TOWER WAS
REPAYRD BY THE
LADIE ANNE
CLIFFORD
COUNTESSES
DOWAGER OF
PEMBROKEE
DORSETT AND
MONTGOMERY
BARONESSE
CLIFFORD
WESTMERLAND

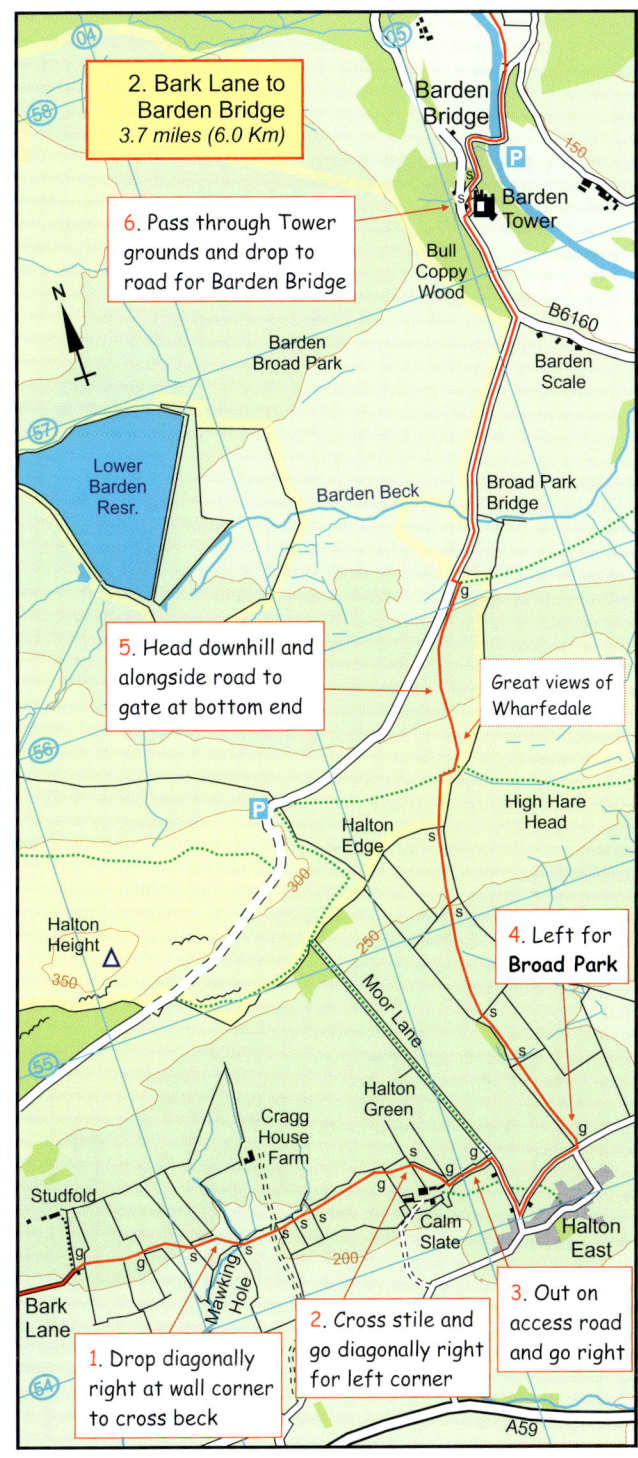

2. Bark Lane to Barden Bridge
3.7 miles (6.0 Km)

6. Pass through Tower grounds and drop to road for Barden Bridge

5. Head downhill and alongside road to gate at bottom end

Great views of Wharfedale

4. Left for **Broad Park**

3. Out on access road and go right

2. Cross stile and go diagonally right for left corner

1. Drop diagonally right at wall corner to cross beck

Barden Tower

This is a stretch of lovely riverside walking, with views of Barden Fell on your right; Simon's Seat at the far end of the fell will remain invisible until you reach Appletreewick. Follow this riverside path for approximately one mile until the path leaves the river alongside Howgill Beck (GR 058592). The path becomes a track beside some farm buildings and eventually comes out onto the road just below Howgill. Turn left here over the bridge and take the track on your left signposted to 'Appletreewick and Burnsall'. The path returns to the river once more and as it enters the woods a touching memorial will be seen low down on your right:

AND VESEIE LADY OF THE HONOR OF SKIPTON IN CRAVEN AND HIGH SHERIFESSE BY INHERITANCE OF THE COUNTIE OF WESTMERLAND IN THE YEARES 1658 AND 1659 AFTER IT HAD LAYNE RUINOUS EVER SINCE ABOUT 1589 WHEN HER MOTHER THEN LAY IN ITT AND WAS GREATE WITH CHILD WITH HER TILL NOWE THAT ITT WAS REPAYRED BY THE SAYD LADY.

ISA.CHAPT. 58. VER. 12. GOD'S NAME BE PRAISED

THE BRADFORD BRANCH OF THE BRITISH SUB-AQUA CLUB HAS FIXED A PLAQUE TO THE ROCK IN THE RIVER TO THE MEMORY OF PAT PROUDFOOT 1942-1960 WHO SAW IN THE NEW YEAR 1960 UNDER WATER HERE BUT DIED ON MAY 23RD. HER FRIENDS WISH TO REMEMBER HER

Beyond the Tower the route turns right down the road to Barden Bridge, built by Lady Anne after her restoration of the Tower. Alternatively you can visit the Tower before dropping down through the field to reach the road and bridge.

Follow the road over the bridge and take the first path on your left between the river and the road. This leads you to the Wharfe's bank, and also a meeting with the Dales Way long distance footpath - an 80 mile walk from Ilkley to Windermere, which has become one of our most popular long distance walks.

Wharfe near Appletreewick

& INVITE THOSE WHO READ THIS TO CONTRIBUTE TO CANCER RESEARCH.

The attractive path takes you walking through leafy woods and past rapids which are very popular with canoeists. The route to Burnsall is very easy to follow as it hugs the riverbank almost all the way. When the path emerges into a grassy area, the village of Appletreewick (locally pronounced Ap'trick) can be seen across the field on your right.

The stone houses of the village are steeped in history, and at one time a fair was held on the land between the river and the village. Ap'trick's claim to fame lies in the story of one of its inhabitants - namely William Craven - born in the village in 1548. As a boy he was apprenticed to a draper, but left home at the age of 14 to make his fortune in London. In this he succeeded, and eventually became Lord Mayor of London in 1610. This incredible rise to fame earned him the nickname 'Dick Whittington of the Dales'.

The field here is used as a car park in the

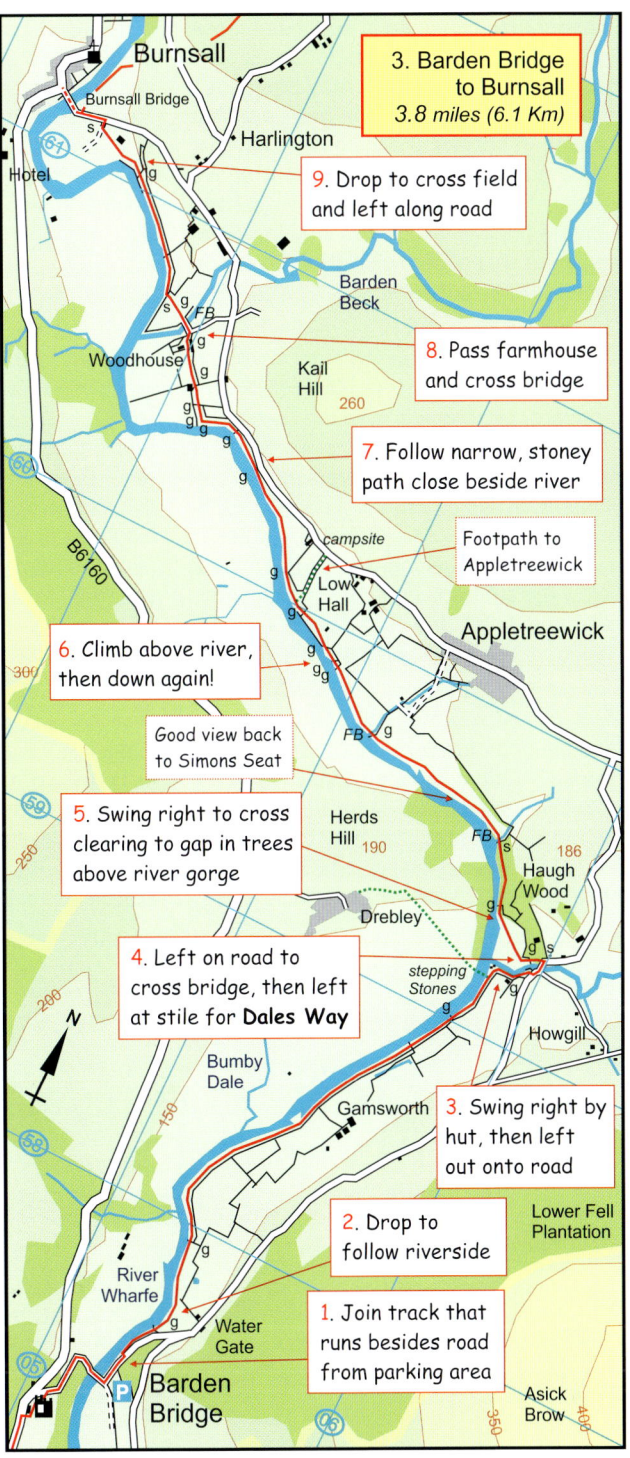

3. Barden Bridge to Burnsall
3.8 miles (6.1 Km)

9. Drop to cross field and left along road

8. Pass farmhouse and cross bridge

7. Follow narrow, stoney path close beside river

6. Climb above river, then down again!

Good view back to Simons Seat

5. Swing right to cross clearing to gap in trees above river gorge

4. Left on road to cross bridge, then left at stile for **Dales Way**

3. Swing right by hut, then left out onto road

2. Drop to follow riverside

1. Join track that runs besides road from parking area

summer months – care is needed at these times to circumvent the footballs and deckchairs, and earplugs may be needed but, no matter, you are only passing through. A backward glance here will give you a good view of Simon's Seat above Barden Fell. A campsite is soon passed which is popular with Dales Way travellers and there are no more official campsites on our route until Kettlewell.

Our route is obvious as it leaves the river for a short distance, bearing right to reach Woodhouse Farm. Go through the farmyard, bearing left over the footbridge and carry on straight ahead to reach a gate which leads you onto a riverside path to Burnsall. In summer this is a tremendously popular spot for picknickers. Burnsall lies in a very attractive setting, nestling as it does below the surrounding fells. It has a shop, cafe and hotel and is a lovely unspoilt village considering its popularity.

However your route doesn't go directly into Burnsall; you must turn left at the road and take the path on your right (directly before Burnsall Bridge) marked 'Skuff Rd'. This path follows the riverside for two fields; on the other side of the river may be seen our fellow Dales Way walkers, whose route we have now left. Leave the second field over a stile and go up the hill ahead of you, passing through ancient plough strips, to reach a gated stile on the skyline and Skuff Road (GR 035614). Cross the road, over a stile and follow the direction of the finger post marked 'Raikes Road' to reach another stile.

Keep the same general direction and take the stile directly ahead of you, ignoring the one on your right to Hartlington Raikes. Cross the next two fields diagonally left, and then follow the fence on the right to a gate which leads to South View Farm (GR 038620). Do not go through the gate but turn left and go diagonally back across the other side of the field and over the stile in the wall on your right. Turn left and follow the fence to a stile in the wall corner. Once over this, turn right and follow the wall on your right to a stile in the wall ahead. Turn left over the stile and follow the wall to a gateway at GR 034621.

A beautiful view of Burnsall can be seen over this wall, whilst away to your right are extensive views of Hebden Moor, and the track known as Backstone Edge Lane is clearly visible on the hillside. Turn diagonally right here across the field whilst keeping well left of a field barn, contour the hillside and drop down to reach a gate at a point where the wall turns dog-leg fashion, with the farm just beyond. Head across the middle of the next field to reach a gate giving access to Ranelands Farm. Pass between some farm buildings, with the farmhouse on your right. Go through a further gate and bear right across the next field to reach a stone step-

Burnsall

stile in the wall ahead. Go over another stile directly opposite, and drop down to a good track.

Turn right here (signed to Hebden) and soon bear left over a little stream to the left of a gate. Follow the now obvious path going over a footbridge beside the weir. Go through a kissing gate ahead of you and follow the path as it contours around the hillside with a stream on your right, soon reaching a stone stile which gives access up the hill to the village of Hebden.

For those of you wishing to end your first day here there is a cafe, B & B's and the Clarendon Hotel, where meals and accommodation are available.

Once a mining village, Hebden's tiny cottages grouped haphazardly beside the beck, used to house the lead miners and their families. The remnants of their mine buildings can be found at the top of Hebden Gill and it is said that as the workers made their way home back down the gill, and if the wind was in the right direction, they could smell their bacon cooking half way down. Lead was mined here at least as far back

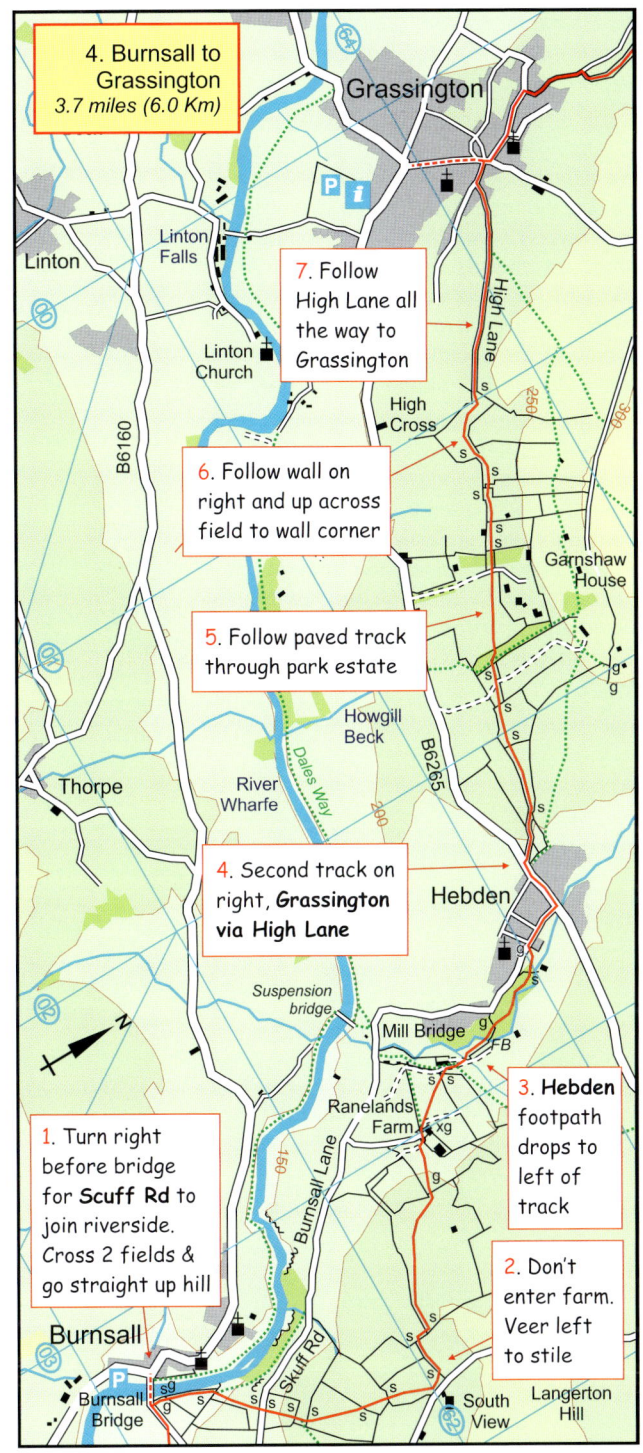

4. Burnsall to Grassington
3.7 miles (6.0 Km)

7. Follow High Lane all the way to Grassington

6. Follow wall on right and up across field to wall corner

5. Follow paved track through park estate

4. Second track on right, **Grassington via High Lane**

3. **Hebden** footpath drops to left of track

2. Don't enter farm. Veer left to stile

1. Turn right before bridge for **Scuff Rd** to join riverside. Cross 2 fields & go straight up hill

21

as Roman times and during that period it was transported, most likely by packhorse, to Boroughbridge for shipping abroad.

The road through Hebden, from Grassington and beyond and heading eastwards, became an important highway. During the medieval period it was used by the monks of Fountains Abbey to transport wool eastwards from their grange at Kilnsey. The wool was transferred to ships at Boroughbridge from where it went down the rivers Ure and Ouse to the Humber and was subsequently exported to Europe.

Leave Hebden village, turning left onto the main B6265 towards Grassington and passing the Clarendon Hotel on your right. Take the second track which opens up on your right, and is signed to 'Grassington'. Follow this over a stile and through three fields to reach a small belt of mainly coniferous trees in the grounds of Garnshaw House (GR 018634).

This was once the site of a sanitorium, but has now been given over to exclusive residential plots and enterprisingly a wildlife meadow. Once over the stile which gives access to the copse, take the central path straight ahead of you – signed 'Grassington'. Follow it through the trees and along the paved trod to reach some ash trees. Beneath these trees and a little to the left is a memorial stone. The inscription on a piece of Millstone Grit states:

WIN CUMMING
THE INFLUENCE OF HER CHARM
WILL NEVER LEAVE THIS PLACE.

Continue along the trod to a tarmac road, cross this and keep on to reach a stile into a field. Cross the next two fields in the same general direction, cross over a track and take the stile ahead into the next field, dropping down to a good track on your left. At the end of this field as the track bears away to the left, carry straight on with a wall on your right. At the wall corner bear right across the next field to reach a further wall corner accompanied by a footpath sign.

Hebden

Grassington

Here you will rejoin the track which leads you over a stile to the right of a gate and into a walled lane known as High Lane.

Stage One is almost ended as Grassington now becomes visible on your left. Lady Anne would have travelled on the other side of the river underneath what is now the B6160 on her journey up the valley, no doubt wearing her customary garb of rough black serge. She was very frugal (hence the serge dress) and there are records of her purchasing such a garment from a tailor in Appleby for 39/6d. She was certainly no trendsetter, as one comment on her apparel proves - 'a dress not disliked by any yet imitated by none'. She often broke her journey at Cuthbert Wade's house in Kilnsey before carrying on through Kettlewelldale.

At the end of High Lane turn right onto the tarmac to reach an area beneath a sycamore tree used for car parking. Cross this area and Grassington town centre is down the road to your left.

Grassington has all amenities, and is a small but bustling town. It is the main shopping centre for the upper dale, and attracts visitors from far and wide with its attractive buildings and cobbled streets. It is particularly popular on any Saturday in December, when a Victorian Fair is held. Many folk dress up in costume, the town is full of stalls selling various seasonal items and there is a marvellous festive atmosphere.

It is also home to a National Park Centre which houses an abundance of information for the visitor. There should be no problems with accommodation here, apart from the lack of a campsite.

As at Hebden, Grassington was once the centre of a flourishing lead-mining industry which had been worked since Pre-Roman times. Remains of this are very much in evidence all over the hillsides to the north of the town.

STAGE TWO: Grassington to Buckden

Distance: 12½ miles   Total distance: 28 miles

Ordnance Survey Maps 1:25,000 -
Explorer OL 2 – Yorkshire Dales South & West
Explorer OL30 – Yorkshire Dales North & Central

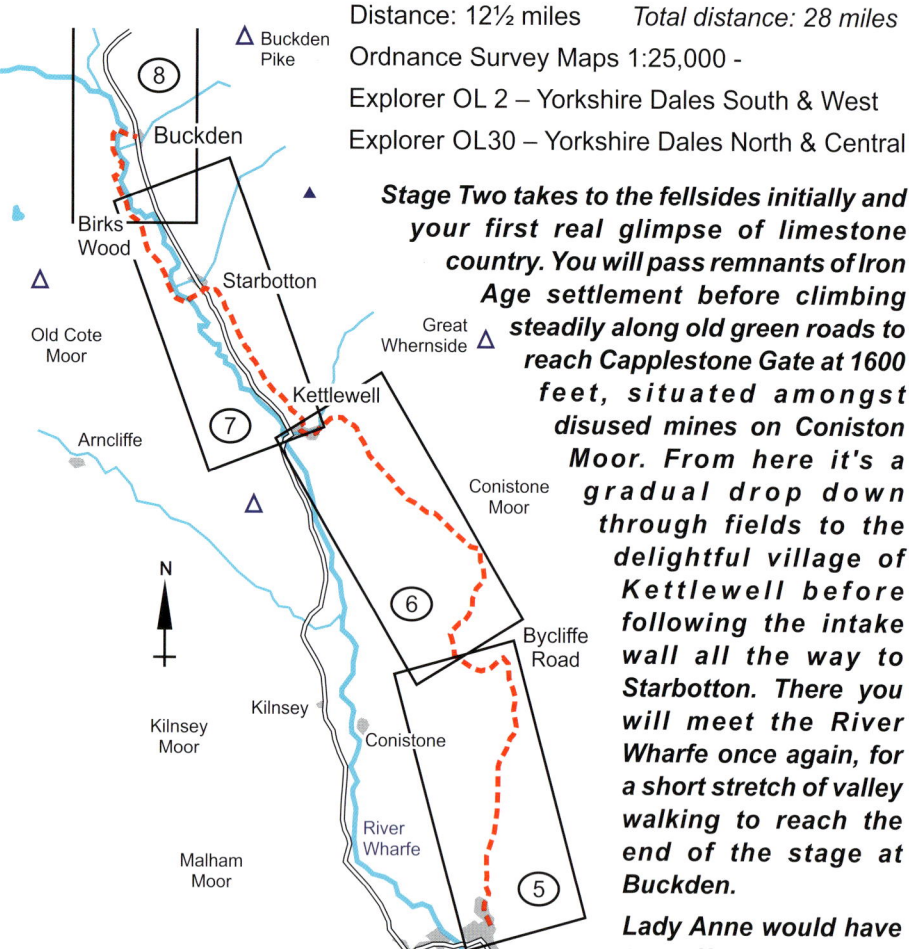

Stage Two takes to the fellsides initially and your first real glimpse of limestone country. You will pass remnants of Iron Age settlement before climbing steadily along old green roads to reach Capplestone Gate at 1600 feet, situated amongst disused mines on Coniston Moor. From here it's a gradual drop down through fields to the delightful village of Kettlewell before following the intake wall all the way to Starbotton. There you will meet the River Wharfe once again, for a short stretch of valley walking to reach the end of the stage at Buckden.

Lady Anne would have travelled along the valley bottom all the way, staying at "Mr. Cuthbert Wade's house in Kilnsey before carrying on the next day thro Kettlewell Dale", but you have the freedom to roam on the fellsides and to savour some of its many delights.

From Grassington return to the junction at the top of the High Street and turn left into Chapel Street. Follow this until you reach Bank Lane on your right, also signed to 'Bycliffe Road'.

Turn along here and the tarmac soon gives way to a good track between stone walls. This shortly turns to the right; ignore the track straight ahead, and carry on right to reach a stile to the left of a gate.

Walk uphill and as the lane opens out, aim for the wall on your right which you must follow to the end of the field. Extensive views can be seen on your left of Wharfedale, with Bastow Wood in the foreground and directly in front of this is the area known as Lea Green – famous for its remains of Iron Age settlements.

At the end of the field pass through a squeeze stile followed by a gated stile - the route is well signposted. Keep on in the same general direction over a series of stiles and heading forever upwards.

Once over a stile at GR 005661 and the start of open access land, take the left fork signed to Bare House.

Shortly you will pass a walled enclosure on your right which is a disused mine shaft. Keep on climbing upwards here, ignoring the path going off left downhill. The ground is light and springy and the walking easy as Littondale comes into view ahead bounded by Hawkswick Moor to the left.

Eventually the path curves round to the right to reach a disused building known as Bare House (GR 005669). Pass through the gate beside the house, where a choice must be made. Your route lies diagonally right towards the corner of a wall - however, if the mist is down, you may choose to follow the path off to the left down towards Conistone. From here a minor road can be followed all the way to Kettlewell.

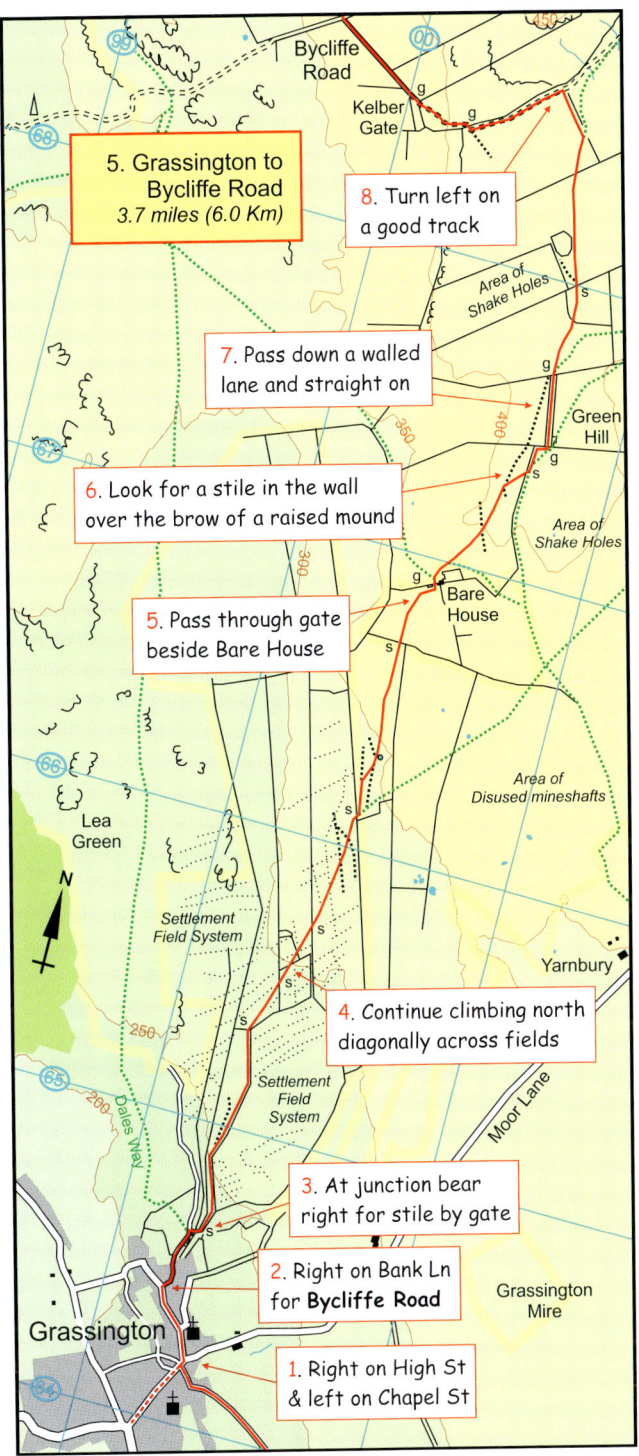

5. Grassington to Bycliffe Road
3.7 miles (6.0 Km)

8. Turn left on a good track
7. Pass down a walled lane and straight on
6. Look for a stile in the wall over the brow of a raised mound
5. Pass through gate beside Bare House
4. Continue climbing north diagonally across fields
3. At junction bear right for stile by gate
2. Right on Bank Ln for **Bycliffe Road**
1. Right on High St & left on Chapel St

Bare House

At the wall corner carry on in the same direction on a cart track ignoring the right fork which follows the wall.

On reaching some raised ground and the remains of an old quarry, take the right fork in the track to reach a gated stile in the wall ahead. This can be a little difficult to find, as the stile is hidden initially by the raised ground.

On the other side of the wall turn left along another cart track as it curves round, eventually reaching a gate which gives access to a walled lane (GR 008675). Ignore the 'Gill House Only' sign, but follow the lane to its end. Pass through the gate and carry on due north to a stile over a wall.

Over to your right is Grassington Moor and an extensive area of disused mines and shafts. Civilization feels a million miles away and it's hard to imagine that this area was ever a hive of activity as it must have been in those far off mining days, for the evidence is all around. Now all is derelict and nature is gradually reclaiming the land and erasing all but the memories.

A vague path meanders in a northerly direction between shafts and shakeholes, passing a fenced off mine shaft on your left before crossing a broken down wall. Keep on until you reach another broken down wall which you follow left to reach a good track, which is Bycliffe Road, at GR 005686. Follow this broad track to the left through two gates, the second of which is known as Kelber Gate. (Eventually the track turns left down to Conistone and another possible bad weather route off the fellside).

At this junction go straight ahead through a gate signed to Capplestone Gate and walk towards a small copse of trees at the wall corner ahead on your right. On reaching this, follow the wall round to the right through a gate. Here a track known as Conistone Turf Road ascends the hillside towards an escarpment.

Eventually you pass through a gap in the wall on your left at the junction of wall and escarpment. Follow the track as it winds uphill towards Capplestone Gate and a trig. point which soon becomes visible on the skyline. Capplestone Gate is used as a checkpoint on the infamous 'Fellsman Hike' - a 62 mile challenge walk held annually by Keighley Scouts. It is one of the toughest walks in the country, involving 11,000 feet of climbing and a lot of peat bogs, but that's another story!

When you reach the top, go through a gate

in the wall signed to Kettlewell, and follow the path left adjacent to a wall; this is marked with yellow posts. Keep straight on, always keeping sight of the wall on your left, until you reach a gate and stile in the wall ahead at GR 999704. The fingerpost over to your right would bring you back to the same place. (If in thick mist, be aware that there is a very large shaft/sink hole just adjacent to the stile.)

Your route lies diagonally downhill now all the way to Kettlewell, but the path can be vague and even non-existent in places. In mist a bearing of 308° takes you to a stile over a wall. Keeping the same general direction, cross a path before going over a further two stiles. In the next field keep on along the main track as it curves left downhill, before curving right to pass beneath an escarpment on your right.

Go over two further stiles and in the next field go over the stile straight ahead - do not be tempted by the gate in the bottom left-hand corner of the field.

Your way lies steeply downhill now as a wall on your left comes into

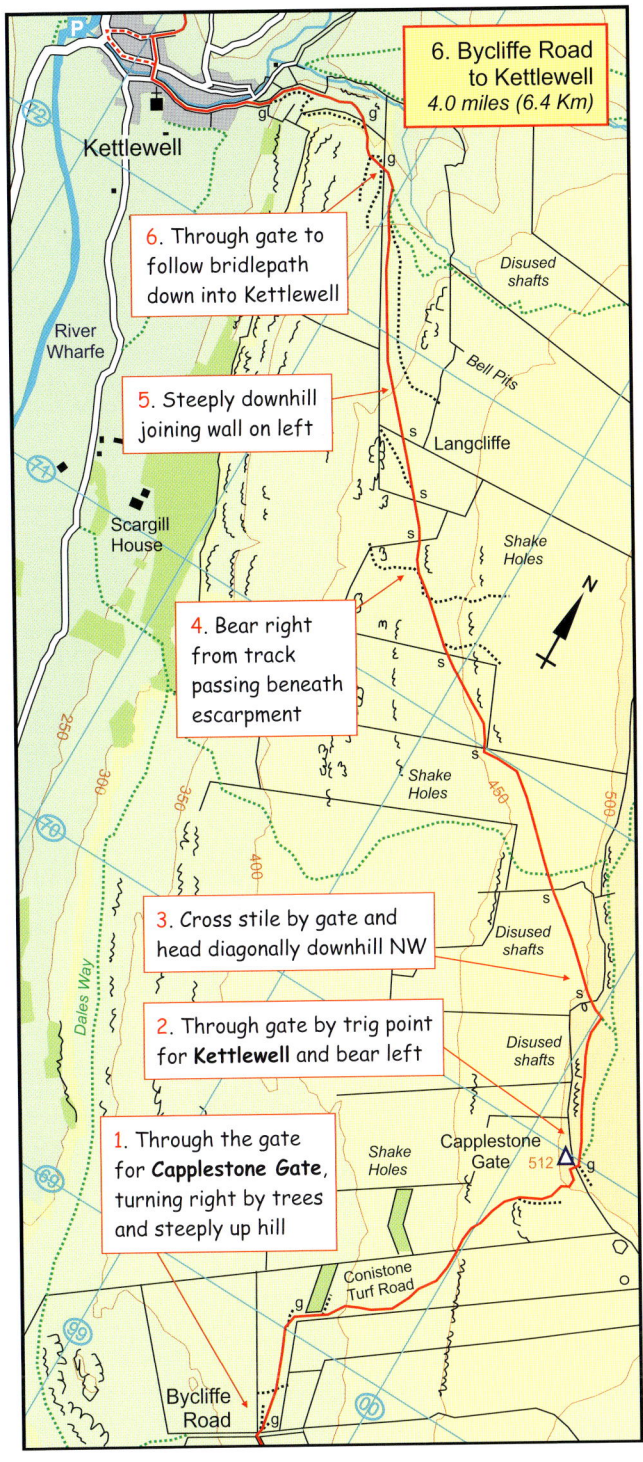

6. Bycliffe Road to Kettlewell
4.0 miles (6.4 Km)

6. Through gate to follow bridlepath down into Kettlewell

5. Steeply downhill joining wall on left

4. Bear right from track passing beneath escarpment

3. Cross stile by gate and head diagonally downhill NW

2. Through gate by trig point for **Kettlewell** and bear left

1. Through the gate for **Capplestone Gate**, turning right by trees and steeply up hill

A corner of Kettlewell

view. Follow this down as two tracks come in from the right.

The track is very clear now and takes you through a gate in the wall on your left and on through another gate with a bridleway sign. The wild and lonely places are now left behind as the houses of Kettlewell come into view. On reaching the road turn left into the village, keeping company with Park Gill Beck on your right as it rushes through the middle of the village on its way to join the river Wharfe. Delightful properties line the banks of the river, many hidden by trees in the height of summer. Follow the road to a junction and the Kings Head pub (if staying here the backpackers amongst you must keep straight on at this point to reach a T-junction. A left turn here will bring you in approximately 200 yards to a campsite where all facilities are available). Otherwise turn right here over the bridge and carry straight on over the crossroads. Those staying in Kettlewell must turn left at this junction - the village is well served with pubs, hotels, shops, B & B accommodation and a youth hostel.

The word Kettlewell means 'stream in the narrow valley' and these natural features, surrounded by high moorland ridges, determined the site of the village in the valley bottom. There were few regular tracks across the moors in Lady Anne's day, most movement being along the valley bottoms which is the route she would have taken. Kettlewell once had a market which was used by the forest people of Langstroth and Litton but this died out at the end of the seventeenth century with disafforestation. Nowadays it is a bubbling, bustling village thronged with people in the summer months and a delight at any time of the year.

Once over the crossroads you will pass the youth hostel on your right before reaching a track on the right with Cam Lodge facing you. Follow the track uphill and through a stile with a wall on your left, and follow the wall as it turns left. Your route is now very straightforward in a north-westerly direction to Starbotton, following the line taken by the river Wharfe in the valley bottom. Keeping the wall always on your left, carry on in the same direction on a very obvious path through a series of stiles. Extensive views of Wharfedale can be seen looking back towards Kettlewell. This is typical Wharfedale scenery, with dry stone walls making fascinating patterns on

Leaving Kettlewell

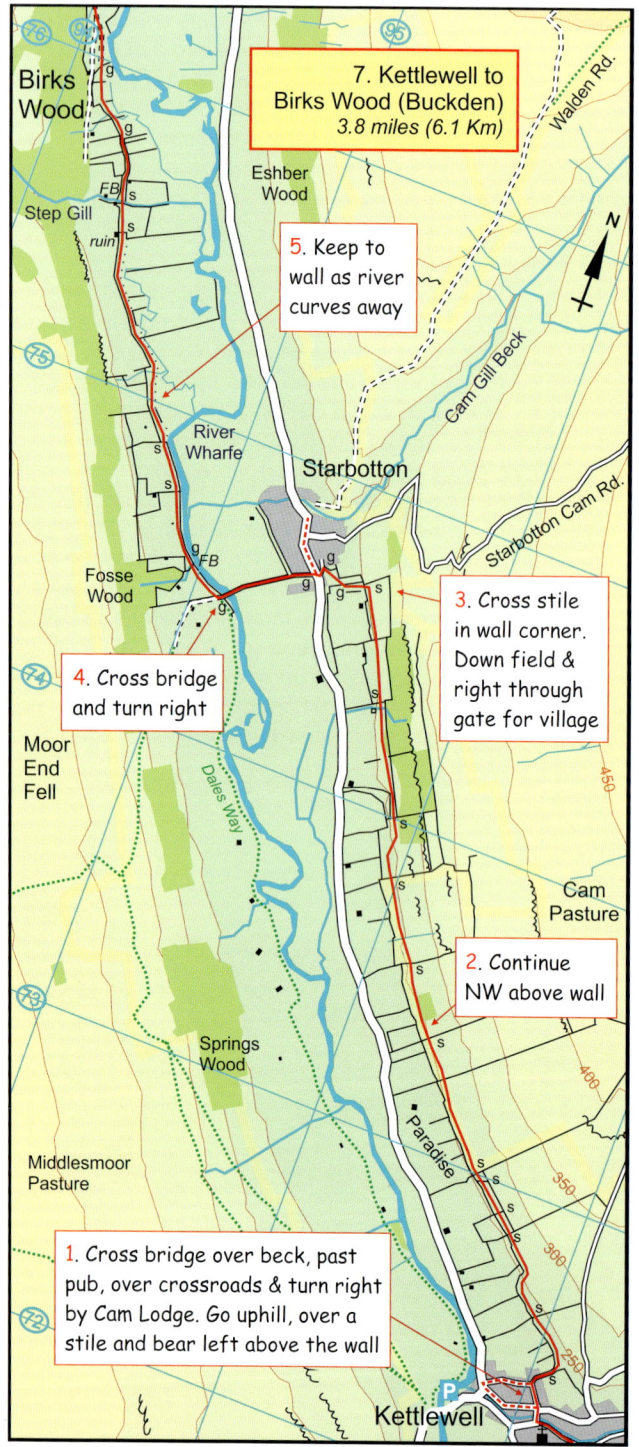

the fellsides.

Eventually Starbotton comes into view, with Chapel Moor at the head of the dale being visible on the horizon.

Shortly before reaching Starbotton you will pass a ruined building on your left. Go through two more fields to find a footpath sign in the wall corner on your left (GR 956747). Go halfway down the field and through a metal gate in the wall on the right, then diagonally down to the village, passing through two fields to reach a metal gate leading onto the road.

Turn left to the B6160 to find a path directly opposite, signed to Buckden. Starbotton is home to the Fox and Hounds pub and two B&Bs, plus camping facilities.

The walled lane takes you down to the river Wharfe and is a delight in summer when wild flowers can be seen in abundance: meadowsweet, meadow cranesbill, sweet cicely and wild campanula to name just a few. Ignore the track on your right and soon you pass over the bridge where a right turn will take you along the riverbank which you follow to Buckden. You

The word Buckden means 'the valley of the bucks' and it was here that the foresters of Langstrothdale Chase lived. The area was heavily wooded and extended high up into Langstrothdale, the upper section of Wharfedale. Buckden itself consisted of a hunting lodge and a few foresters' dwellings. Members of the Clifford family hunted red deer here at the beginning of the seventeenth century, and leased a farm at Hubberholme (just over a mile away) whilst reserving fishing, hunting and hawking rights for themselves.

Hubberholme itself is worth a visit if you have time on your hands. The George Inn serves food and the church houses a famous rood loft of medieval origin. The remainder of the woodwork was replaced in the first half of the twentieth century by Robert Thompson of Kilburn, whose mouse trademark can be found somewhere on every piece of his work; it can be quite enjoyable searching through the church furniture for these. J.B. Priestley was so enthralled by the church and its setting that he arranged to have his remains interred here.

Buckden Pike is the hill rising up behind Buckden and it was here that lead ore was mined until the late nineteenth century. Close to the trig. point on the Pike is a stone cross which stands as a memorial to a Polish aircrew; their aeroplane crashed in heavy snow during the Second World War and only one man survived. He had a broken leg but somehow managed to crawl away in search of help; he came across a fox's footprints in the snow and, reasoning that the fox would be heading for food in the valley bottom, decided to follow the prints and eventually reached safety at Cray.

To commemorate his escape he had the cross erected, which features the bronze head of a fox set into its concrete base.

The Buck Inn at Buckden is probably of 16th. century origin and was once used for the auctioning of sheep fleeces. At Christmas it is host to the traditional 'Three Inns Walk', when residents walk from the Buck to the White Lion at Cray and then onto the George at Hubberholme before returning to Buckden for Christmas Dinner!

Buckden Village Store

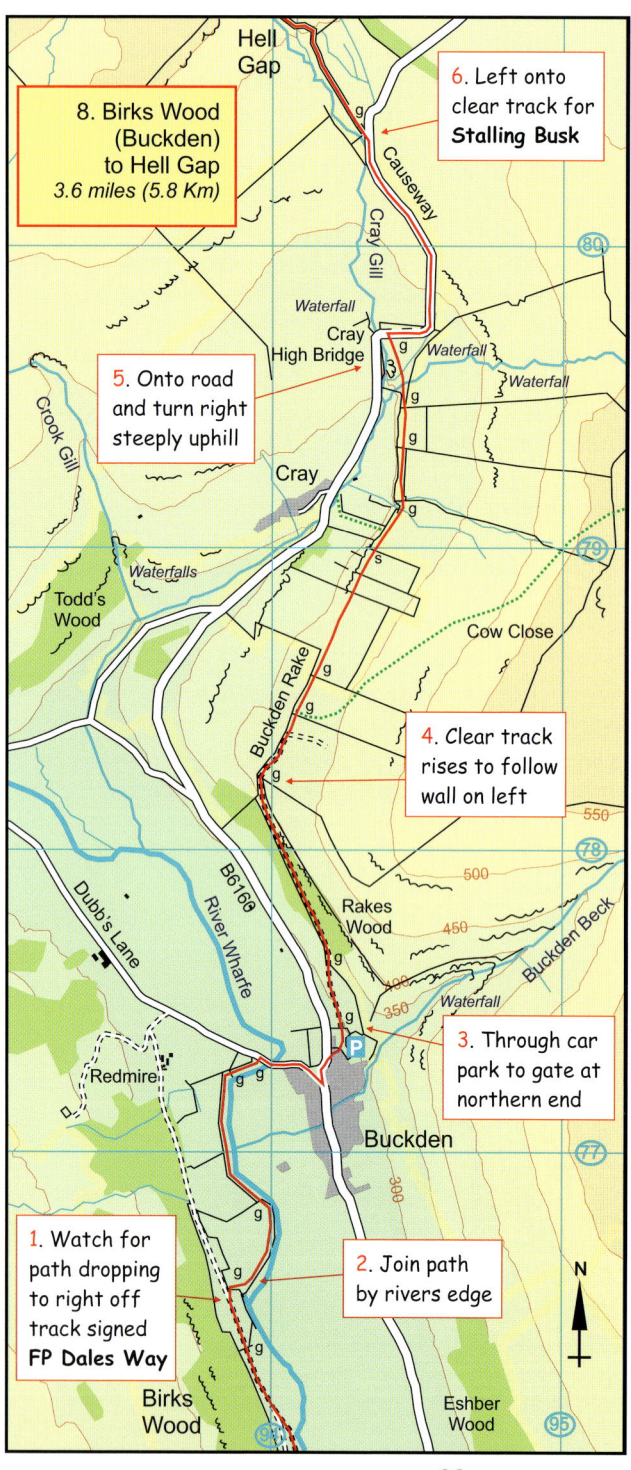

are once again treading the same footsteps as the Dales Way travellers. Soon the river loops away to the right but your route carries straight on. There are intermittent yellow dots marking the way - do not be tempted to stray off to the right as the ground here can be very marshy.

Eventually you reach a good track beneath Birks Wood and the village of Buckden comes into view ahead. Approximately 100 yards after passing a large barn on the left (GR 939764) a 'Dales Way' sign will be seen on your right pointing the way down to the riverbank. This is followed all the way to Dubb's Lane. On reaching the lane, turn right over the bridge to enter Buckden.

The village has a shop (limited opening hours), the Buck Inn and a B&B. There's also a camp site with camping pods available.

STAGE THREE: Buckden to Hawes

Distance: 18 miles   *Total distance: 46 miles*

Ordnance Survey Maps 1:25,000 -

Explorer OL30 – Yorkshire Dales North & Central

The route takes to the high ground initially with a steep climb to reach the top of Stake Moss, then follows lovely walking on good tracks with extensive views all the way down to Carpley Green on the flanks of Addlebrough. These ancient tracks will take you out of Wharfedale over Stake Allotments into Wensleydale, where you will pass Nappa Hall with its associations with Lady Anne. Then commences a valley walk to reach the delightful town of Askrigg, famed for its connections with the television programme 'All Creatures Great and Small', before carrying on through fields and pastures to reach the market town of Hawes and the end of Stage Three.

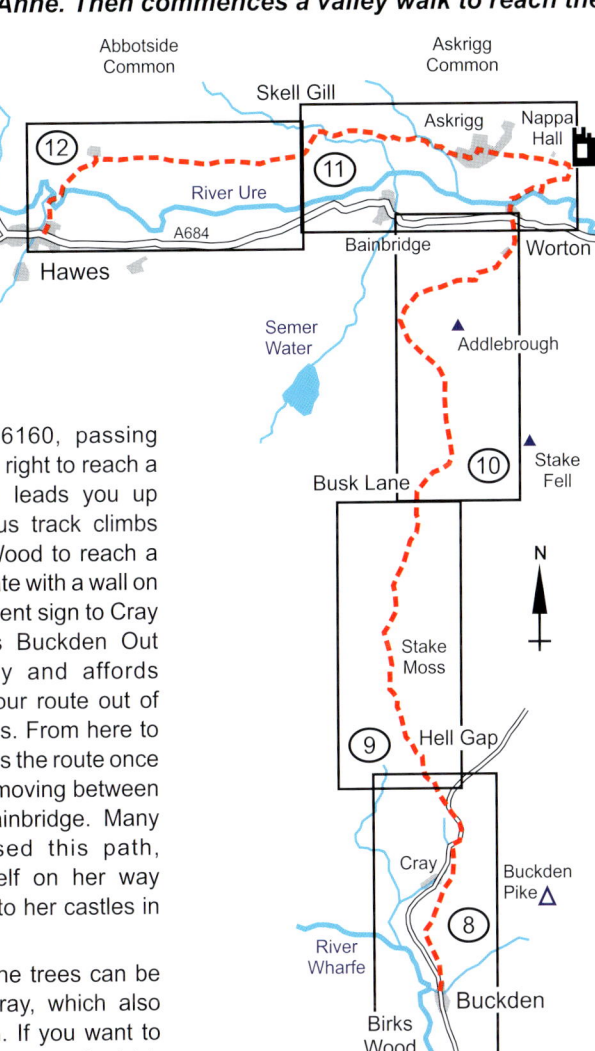

Leave Buckden on the B6160, passing through the car park on your right to reach a gate at the far side which leads you up Buckden Rake. This obvious track climbs gradually above Buckden Wood to reach a gate. Keep on through the gate with a wall on your left following a subsequent sign to Cray Bridge. The path contours Buckden Out Moor, is soft and springy and affords excellent views ahead of your route out of Wharfedale over Stake Moss. From here to the Moss and a little beyond is the route once used by the Romans when moving between their forts at Ilkley and Bainbridge. Many travellers have since used this path, including Lady Anne herself on her way through the Dales en route to her castles in the Eden Valley.

Over to your left amongst the trees can be seen the tiny hamlet of Cray, which also includes the White Lion Inn. If you want to visit Cray, look for a sign on your left which

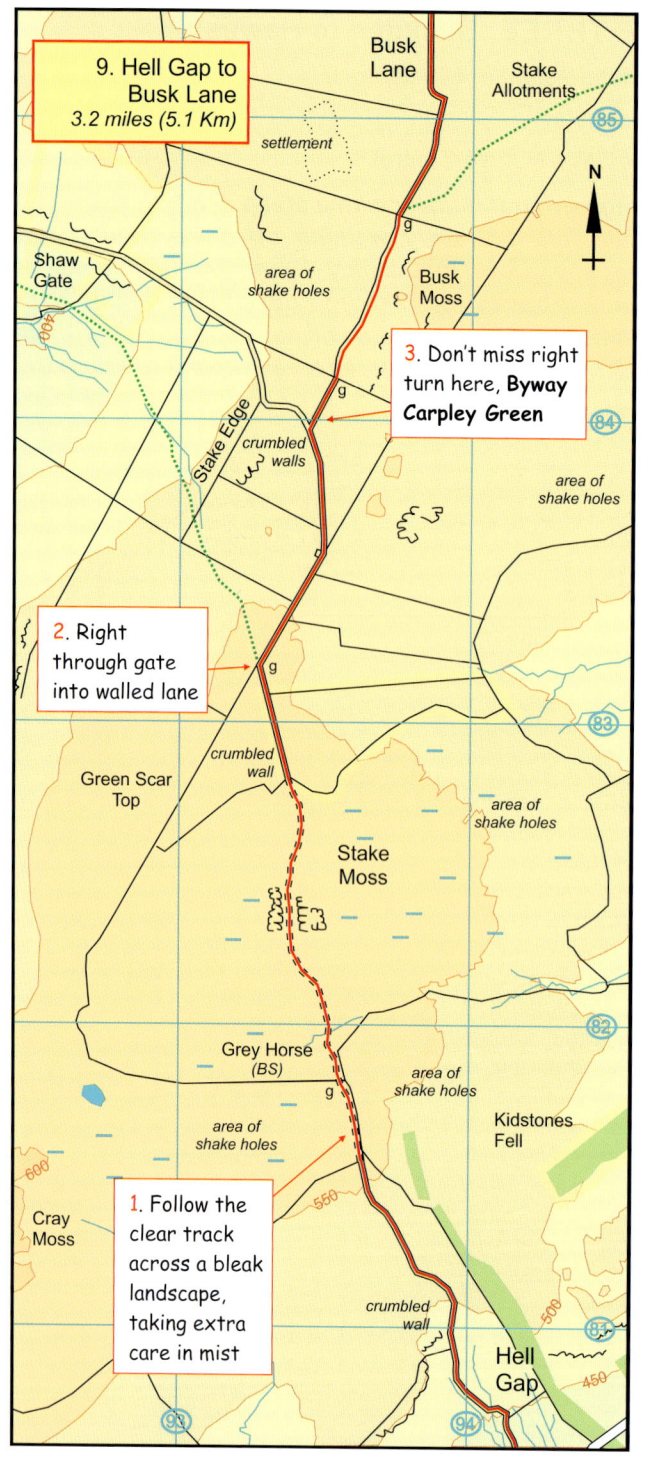

will take you down the fellside to the inn; your route can be picked up again by carrying on along the road to Cray High Bridge (GR 944797). Otherwise continue straight ahead, keeping the wall on your left until you come out into open ground. In times of heavy rainfall, impressive waterfalls cascade over the limestone around here. The path then crosses this last field to reach the road at Cray High Bridge. Turn right and follow the road for just over half a mile until you reach an area of hard standing on the left. This leads you through a gate and so onto an excellent track known as Gilbert Lane and signed to Stalling Busk. The track starts rising quite soon, taking you up through Hell Gap and eventually onto Stake Moss.

This is an empty, featureless landscape which in bad weather can appear very bleak and inhospitable. Perhaps you may care to identify with some of Lady Anne's tenants, as they trudged along in the mud whilst her women servants sat back in the relative comfort of a coach drawn by horses.

Comfort is possibly the wrong word to use here, as the roads in the seventeenth century were exceedingly rough, particularly in wet weather, and the coaches would not be very well sprung. As for Lady Anne, she preferred to travel in a horse litter, a carriage slung between two horses. This must also have been a very rough ride and certainly not for the fainthearted or those inclined to be seasick!

The route is obvious, with walls intermittently, as you cross the watershed and eventually reach a point at GR 932832 where the track veers to the right at a boundary wall. Go through the gate here to enter a walled lane. You have now left the peat hags behind and the landscape changes once more with dry stone walls patterning the fellsides again. In just over half a mile at GR 934840 a broad track will be seen on your right with broken down walls on either side and signed to Carpley Green. Take care not to miss this as I did once whilst busy chatting, otherwise you will end up in the valley of Raydale above Semerwater.

About 200 yards along this track is a gate in the wall ahead which can be seen from the junction. Go through this and you are now on Busk Lane which will take you after approximately 2½ miles to a group of farm buildings known as Carpley Green. There is once again good walking to be had along here, often between ruined dry stone walls and with no problems of route finding. Very soon a dramatic view of Addlebrough reveals itself as you come over the brow of a hill. This flat topped elevation was an ancient hill fort in Roman times and its unmistakable shape dominates the landscape.

At Carpley Green you reach a metalled road which you must follow for just short of a mile. On the hillside to your left are the remains of a Roman road known as Cam High Road, which stretches from Bainbridge to Ribblehead and originally continued on to Ingleton. Nestling beneath the High Road, in the valley of Raydale, lies Semerwater, which 3000 years ago housed lake dwellings. As the lake comes into view on your left, the road curves to the

Carpley Green & Addlebrough

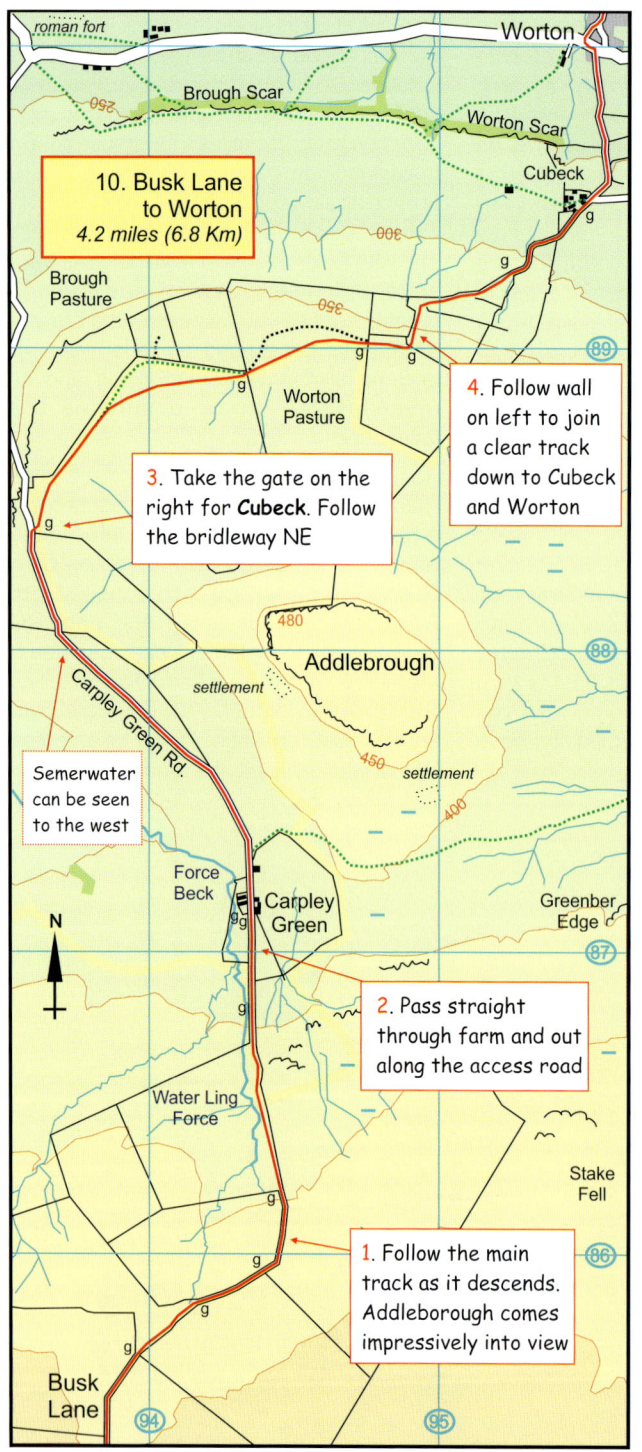

right and starts to descend at GR 935883. About 100 yards along here on the right will be seen a gate at GR 936884 and a sign to Cubeck.

Go through the gate and follow the grassy path in a north-easterly direction to meet a wall coming in on your left. Carry straight on with the wall in sight on your left. Eventually you reach a gateway across your path which gives access to an open area. The wall drops away left as does a tempting path which you must disregard and walk straight on across the field towards a gateway in the far wall ahead of you. Once through this, keep to the same direction until you reach a wall corner (GR 949890) where a left turn through the gate will lead you to a track which descends the hillside.

Ahead of you extensive views of Wensleydale begin to unfold, Askrigg can be seen in the valley bottom and to the right of it lies Nappa Hall which is your next destination. The track curves to the right through a metal gate and carries on to reach the hamlet of Cubeck. On reaching a tarmac road turn left and follow it downhill for a quarter of a mile to the village of Worton.

On reaching the main road turn left and then take the first turning right. An inscription can be seen on this first building on the right, above the window, put there one assumes by the original builder:

> MICHAEL SMITH
> MECHANICK
> BUT HE THAT
> BUILT ALL THINGS
> IS GOD.   Heb 3

Follow the road through the village and down to the riverbank. As you approach the River Ure, Nappa Hall comes into view again on the hillside ahead. Cross the river by the bridge and as the road swings sharp left, take the path on your right signed to Aysgarth. Follow the path beside the river, crossing footbridges and a stile before reaching Nappa Mill. Turn left here along an unmetalled road to reach a little bridge which you do not cross, taking the stile in

Nappa Hall

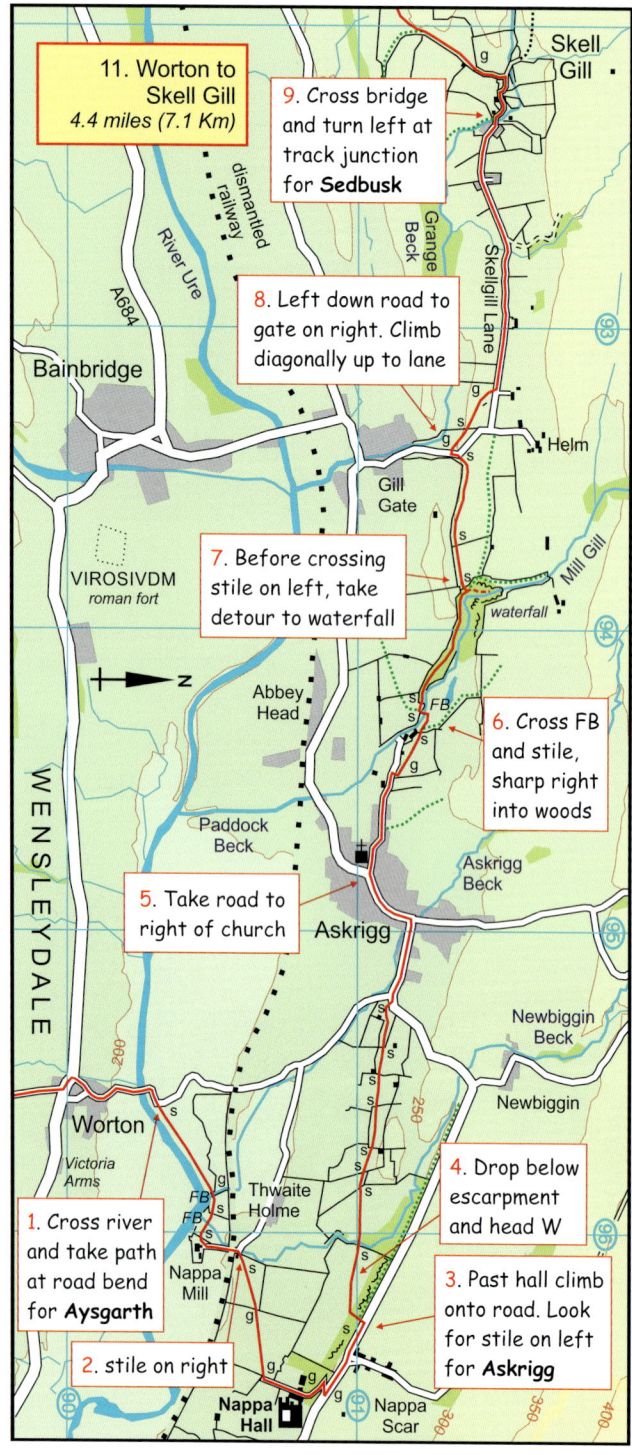

the wall in front of you instead. Your path can clearly be seen as it climbs diagonally right, up the hillside to a gate in the far corner. Cross the next field in the same direction to reach a gate, opening into a lane which takes you left to Nappa Hall.

Nappa Hall is a well preserved medieval building and one of the best examples of its type in the Yorkshire Dales. The pele tower is of particular interest, built between 1450 and 1459 and used for protection against the marauding Scots. The hall was built and owned by the Metcalfe family who were wealthy landowners, famous for their herd of white horses. Thomas Metcalfe was cousin to Lady Anne, and his home became a resting place for her after her travels over the Stake Pass. Her famous diaries record a journey taken in October 1663 when she left Skipton Castle:

"did I remove from thence onwards on my journie towards Westmerland, so as I went to Mr. Cuthbert Wades House in Kilnsey and lay there that night. And the next day from thence *through Kettlewelldale, upp Buckden Rakes and over the Staks into Wensleydale to my Cozen Mr. Thomas Metcalfes house at Nappa Hall, where I lay also that night".*

Other visitors to Nappa included James 1 and Sir Walter Raleigh; Mary Queen of Scots also stayed for two nights after her escape over Leyburn Shawl had failed.

Follow the track past the hall and up the hill to reach the road (GR 965909). Turn left and, after passing a turning to the right to Nappa Scar, look for a footpath sign on your left marked 'Askrigg ¾ mile'. Walk straight ahead to reach a path taking you down below the escarpment, where you need to walk diagonally right in a westerly direction to a stile in a wall ahead (GR 961910). The wall is hidden until the last 50 yards, but two prominent sycamore trees before it may help to guide you. Cross the stream at a convenient spot and scramble uphill in a westerly direction heading for the middle one of three telegraph poles uphill ahead of you.

As you reach the brow of the hill look for a gate atop a stile in the wall ahead. Once over this, keep to the same direction with the wall on your right to reach a further stile where Askrigg can be seen in front of you. Carry on through gates and stiles to reach the road. Turn left along the main road to reach Askrigg, turning left at the T-junction to reach the centre. For those stopping overnight here there is a shop, cafes, B & B's, hotels and a limited bus service.

Askrigg is famous in modern times for the building known as Crinkley House near the church, which was used extensively by the BBC for the series 'All Creatures Great and Small'. The town is a gem of a spot with an old market cross set amongst cobbles in the market place and flanked by the thirteenth century parish church. In its heyday Askrigg was a thriving market town until Hawes received its own charter in 1699, when its importance as a trading town went into decline. During the eighteenth century one of its main industries was clock making and it is said that there were more clocks made in

Askrigg

Askrigg & Addlebrough

Askrigg than anywhere else in the North Riding.

Turner, the painter, stayed at the King's Arms and visited Mill Gill Force which is on your route out of town. Turner would travel on horseback, staying at inns from where he would walk to sites of interest nearby. He filled numerous sketch books with drawings of nearly all the local towns, villages, castles, waterfalls and other points of interest which would be used in his paintings. Yet another great traveller in the vein of Lady Anne!

On leaving Askrigg take the lane to the right of the church. Follow the road round until the tarmac gives way to a track. Soon you will reach a gate with a sign directing you right through the fields to Mill Gill Force. The route is well marked past the old mill, over a tiny bridge and up through the trees high above the river. Here in early summer the banks are carpeted with wild garlic and bluebells, whilst amongst the tangled undergrowth by the beckside remnants of the early Industrial Revolution can be seen slowly decaying.

Eventually you will come to a junction and a sign to the right to 'Mill Gill Fall Only' (GR 939913). It is well worth the few yards walk along this path to visit the falls as they are a

Mill Gill Force

very impressive sight, particularly when the water is in full spate. Your route lies over the stile in the wall on your left: ignore the path straight ahead to Whitfield Gill. Follow a broad track alongside a wall on your left all the way to the road.

Turn left on the road and pass through the gate almost immediately on your right, crossing this field to a stile in the wall ahead. Then head diagonally uphill, passing either side of a short stretch of drystone wall before reaching a gate in the far corner of the field which takes you out onto Skellgill Lane. Turn left here and follow the lane for about half a mile to the hamlet of Skell Gill. The hamlet now appears set in a time warp but during the packhorse days it was a hive of activity and sported three inns, although it is difficult to imagine it now.

Pass through Skell Gill, going over a narrow packhorse bridge to enter a walled track. Take the lane off to your left, don't carry straight on to ford the stream. Keep ahead with the wall on your left and when this wall swings away to the left, look for a broad, indistinct green track which swings away right in a south-westerly direction and signed to Sedbusk. Once over the slight rise aim for a barn and a clump of trees over to your right. As you reach the clump of trees with the farm on your left the path becomes well defined, passing through several fields and always with the wall on your left.

When you reach West Shaw Cote (GR 908910) follow the Permissive Footpath signs which direct you round the farmyard. Eventually you rejoin the original track just beyond the farm, with a wall again on your left.

Soon you enter a walled track and when the track swings left, you will see a stile on the right next to a metal gate. Go over this to enter the fields and, keeping the same westerly direction with a wall on your left, carry on through the fields to reach Litherskew. Most of the traditional stone barns are sadly now redundant and many can be seen crumbling away along this stretch. Cross the track at Litherskew and go straight ahead between a group of buildings. Beyond the last cottage and garage on your right, you'll find a squeeze stile giving access to fields once more.

The path is visible once more and is easy to follow through fields and stiles to Sedbusk. Hawes, the end of Stage Three, can clearly be seen over to the left nestling beneath Wether Fell.

Just short of Sedbusk you will reach a stile

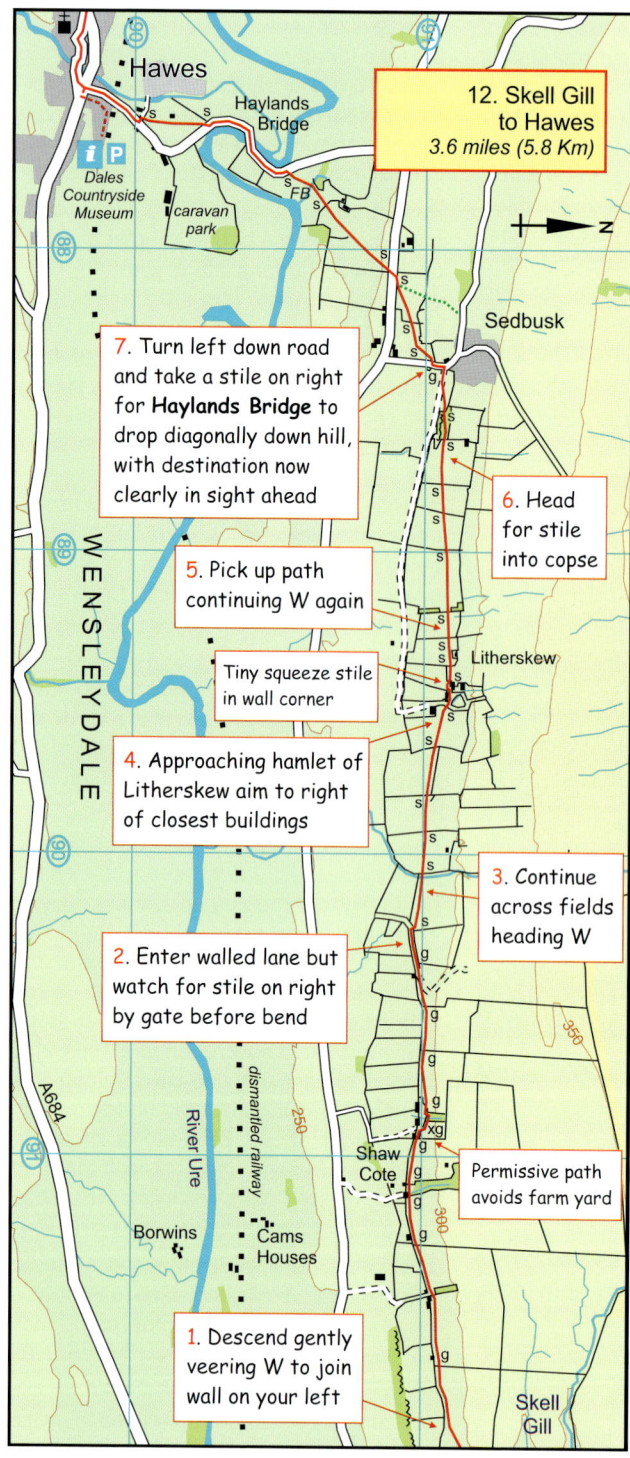

into a copse. Go through the copse and keep on with a wall on your right to reach Sedbusk. Turn left at the road and follow it downhill to reach a footpath on your right. Your route is clearly visible, going diagonally downhill across two fields to meet a minor road.

Cross this and go over the stile ahead. Keeping the same direction, cross further fields towards Hawes and the river Ure. Turn left at the road, cross Haylands Bridge and take the path on your left to avoid traffic. Cross the road and take the short cut on the right along a paved path into Hawes.

Hawes has every amenity: pubs, cafes, a chip shop and several walking shops where gear can be renewed if necessary. There is plenty of accommodation, including a campsite approximately half a mile from the centre at Bainbridge Ings. The site marked on the OS map by the river (GR 879903) is for caravans only.

Hawes

Hawes is the capital of the upper dale and one of the highest market towns in England, famous for its cheese, its working ropemakers and its excellent Dales Countryside Museum. The name Hawes means a neck or pass between mountains and its position near the head of the dale ensures that all roads lead to it. At the east end of town is a narrow bridge under which flows Gayle Beck, making a fascinating sight as it rushes over a series of falls. Few people walk over this bridge without pausing for a moment or two to look over the edge, such is the power of water to arrest our attention.

There has been a market in Hawes for less than 300 years, which makes it quite young by some standards, yet there is a timelessness about the place. It was a centre for the Quaker movement in the seventeenth and eighteenth centuries and the meeting house can be seen near the old station. In the main street, standing back a little from the other houses, can be seen a Quaker rest-house with an inscription above the door:

ANO DOM 1668   GOD BEING WITH US WHO CAN BE AGAINST

The late nineteenth and early twentieth century saw extensive quarrying and mining in the area, a lot of the stone for the big industrial cities of the North West being quarried from here. Evidence of this can be seen in the hills around the town, particularily on the slopes of Great Shunner Fell to the north, which is on the route of the Pennine Way. Hardraw, to the north of the river Ure, is famous for its waterfall which was very popular with the Victorians. It was visited by Wordsworth and his sister Dorothy, and also earlier in the century by Turner during his exploration of the dale. The falls are reached through the Green Dragon Hotel (a small fee is charged) and are quite spectacular at any time, being the largest unbroken waterfall in England.

STAGE FOUR: Hawes to Kirkby Stephen

Distance: 17¼ miles   *Total distance: 63¼ miles*
Ordnance Survey Maps 1:25,000 -
Explorer OL30 – Yorkshire Dales North & Central
Explorer OL19 – Howgill Fells & Upper Eden Valley

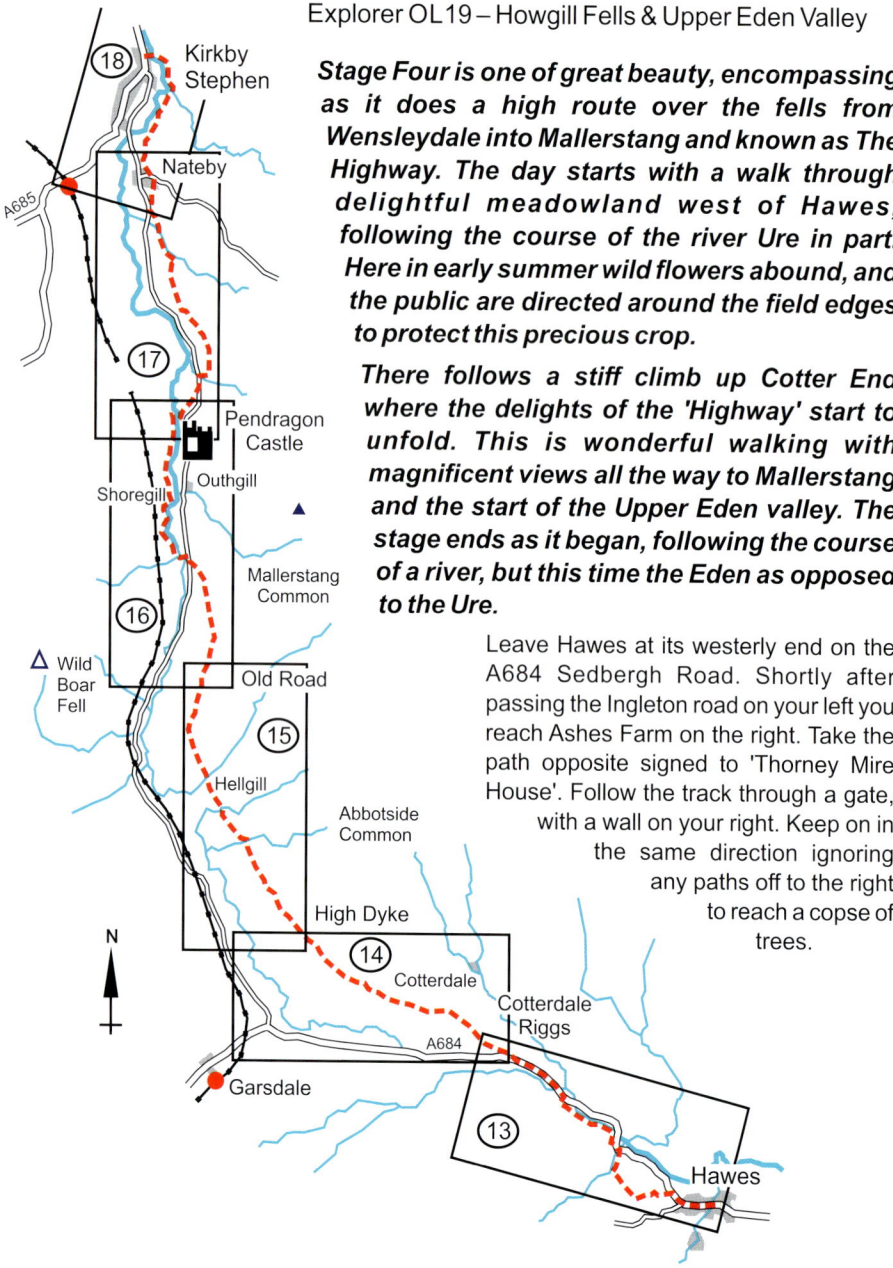

Stage Four is one of great beauty, encompassing as it does a high route over the fells from Wensleydale into Mallerstang and known as The Highway. The day starts with a walk through delightful meadowland west of Hawes, following the course of the river Ure in part. Here in early summer wild flowers abound, and the public are directed around the field edges to protect this precious crop.

There follows a stiff climb up Cotter End where the delights of the 'Highway' start to unfold. This is wonderful walking with magnificent views all the way to Mallerstang and the start of the Upper Eden valley. The stage ends as it began, following the course of a river, but this time the Eden as opposed to the Ure.

Leave Hawes at its westerly end on the A684 Sedbergh Road. Shortly after passing the Ingleton road on your left you reach Ashes Farm on the right. Take the path opposite signed to 'Thorney Mire House'. Follow the track through a gate, with a wall on your right. Keep on in the same direction ignoring any paths off to the right to reach a copse of trees.

Over a stile beyond the copse, cross the next field. In the following one a stone barn is seen ahead. Pass to the left of the barn (GR861899) and in this next field walk diagonally right towards a gate in the far corner. Your next destination of Cotter End is clearly visible on the hillside ahead of you.

Carry on in the same direction over the brow of the hill, keeping a copse of trees and a stone barn away to your left. Your route is all waymarked as you make your way towards Appersett Viaduct. Go over a stile in the wall ahead, and carry on to reach a gate in the left corner of the field adjacent to the viaduct. Turn right along the road and follow it for approximately half a mile until you reach Appersett. In early summer the verges here abound with wild flowers, including sweet cicley and wild garlic. You are accompanied by the sound of Widdale Beck as it rushes to meet the river Ure.

At the T junction turn left and follow the road over the bridge on Widdale Beck, until you reach a stile in the wall on your left signed to Mossdale Head. Once over this

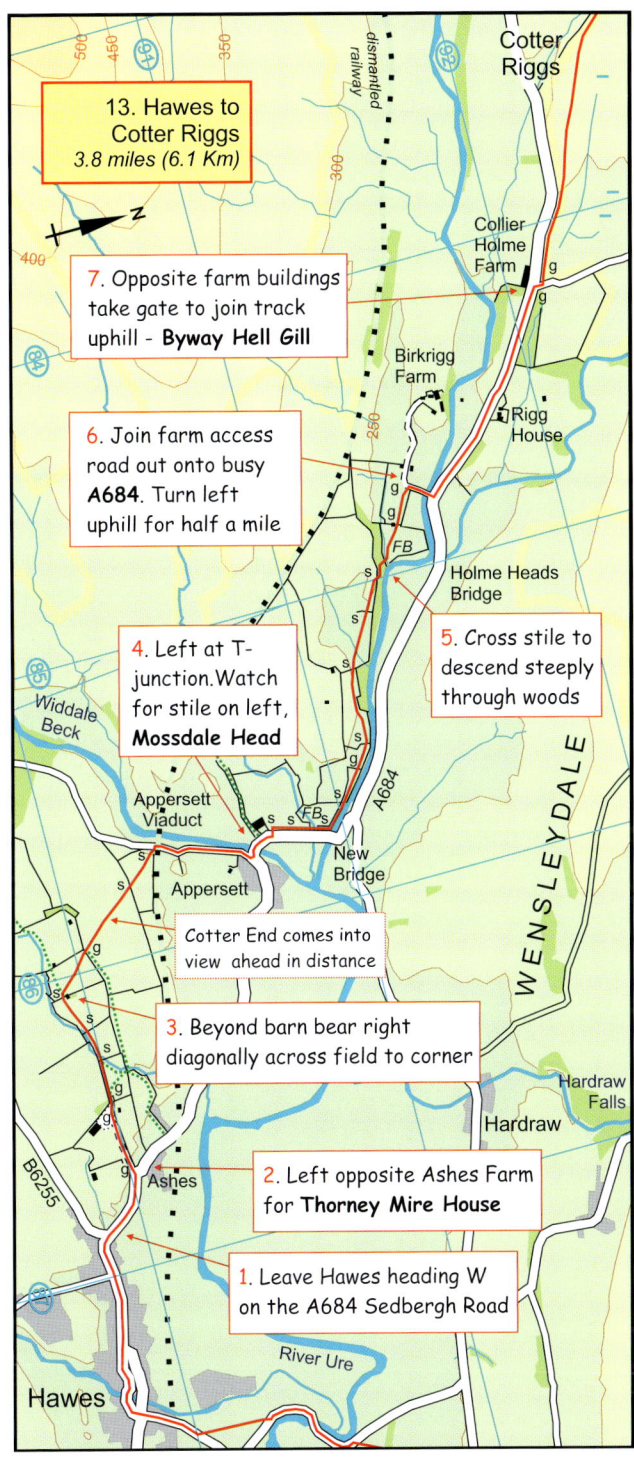

13. Hawes to Cotter Riggs
3.8 miles (6.1 Km)

7. Opposite farm buildings take gate to join track uphill - **Byway Hell Gill**

6. Join farm access road out onto busy **A684**. Turn left uphill for half a mile

5. Cross stile to descend steeply through woods

4. Left at T-junction. Watch for stile on left, **Mossdale Head**

Cotter End comes into view ahead in distance

3. Beyond barn bear right diagonally across field to corner

2. Left opposite Ashes Farm for **Thorney Mire House**

1. Leave Hawes heading W on the A684 Sedbergh Road

turn right, following the direction of the sign to reach the riverbank. The path turns left here to follow the Ure upstream. Keep on beside the river over stiles/gates until you reach a wood and can go no further. Head left uphill beside the wood to a wall corner and follow it round. With the wall on your right, keep on over a ladder stile and then aim diagonally right towards another wall, once again go over a stile ahead of you to eventually reach a step stile in the wall on your right (GR 850913). The path now drops down through the trees to a little beck.

Once over the beck cross the field diagonally left towards a stone barn, and pass through the gate to the right of it. (In high summer you will need to go round the perimeter of the next two wild flower meadows). Cross the next field, and just before reaching another barn you will see a little gate on your right in the corner of the field. This gives access onto a farm track where a right turn will take you over the river Ure and out onto the Sedbergh road. Turn left here and follow the road for approximately half a mile to reach the start of the 'Highway'.

The pasture land is now left behind as you head for the wilder places. You must say farewell to Wensleydale too, for the 'Highway' will take you from the flanks of Abbotside Common and the county of Yorkshire into Mallerstang, the upper Eden and the county of Cumbria. Turn right when you reach a sign to Cotterdale and immediately left is a byway sign to Helgill (once known as Lady Anne Clifford's Highway.)

The 'Highway' was almost certainly a pre-historic route, later used by the Romans. In the eighteenth century it became a major packhorse route, bringing goods from Wensleydale to the busy market town of Kendal and was also used by the drovers coming down from Scotland to the markets in the Dales. Lady Anne used it on her way from Wensleydale into Westmorland to visit Pendragon Castle. We have notes from her diaries to this effect: "from thence I went over Cotter in my coach (where I think never coach went before) and over Hellgill Bridge into Westmerland, so by the Chappell of Mallerstang (I lately repayred) I went into this Pendragon Castle to lye in it again".

Approaching Appersett Viaduct, west of Hawes, with Cotter Riggs beyond

The route is obvious all the way up Cotter End, in mist a wall on your left would act as a guide as it accompanies the path almost all the way to the top. This is the only real hill of the day and the rewards are tremendous, with six miles of superb walking once the top is reached. At the top pass through the gate where an old limekiln will be seen ahead of you; above this a rocky escarpment provides a useful spot to pause and look back on your route out of Wensleydale (there's even a seat!). Hawes can be seen in the foreground and beyond, the unmistakable shape of Addlebrough in the far distance.

Once over the brow of Cotter End, this for me is the start of the 'Highway' proper with good walking, a lot of it on grassy turf and with superb views all around. The route is on a ledge by Abbotside Common all the way to Hell Gill Bridge - a distance of about 3½ miles, and follows a wall on your left for most of the way.

Away to your left is seen Dandrymire Viaduct at Garsdale Head, which carries the famous Settle to Carlisle Railway. Passenger

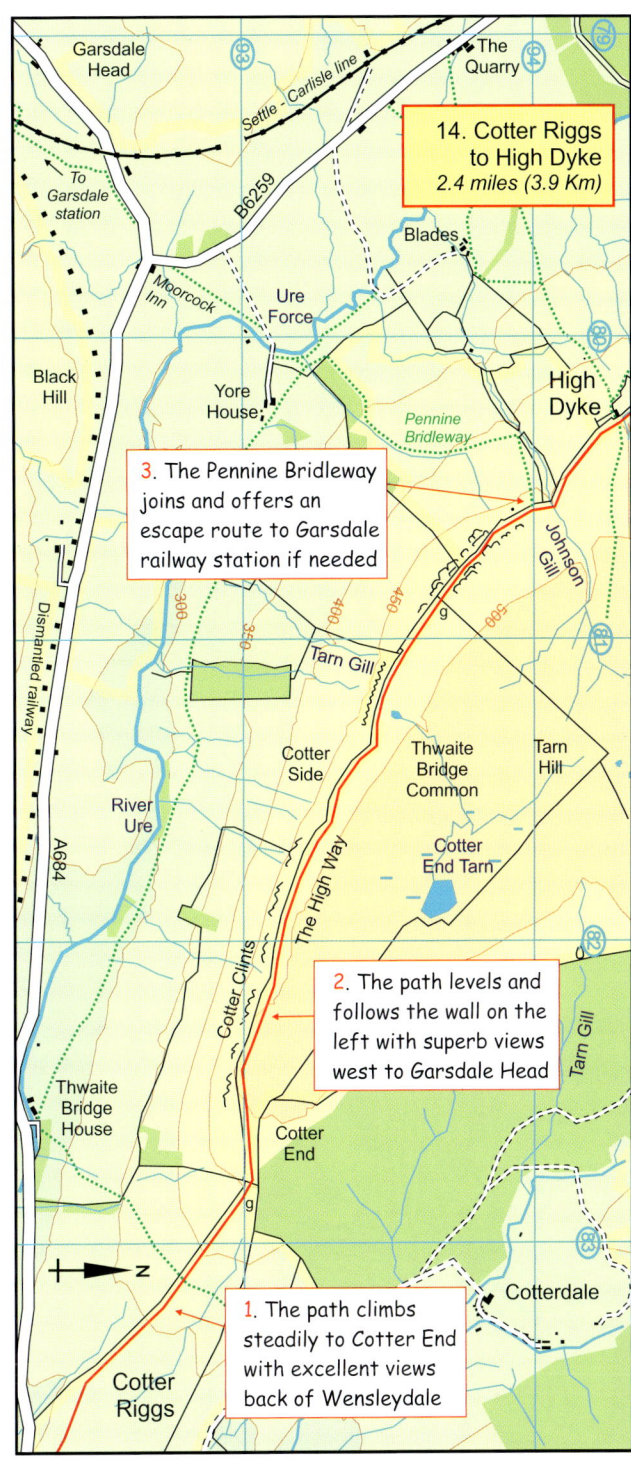

14. Cotter Riggs to High Dyke
2.4 miles (3.9 Km)

3. The Pennine Bridleway joins and offers an escape route to Garsdale railway station if needed

2. The path levels and follows the wall on the left with superb views west to Garsdale Head

1. The path climbs steadily to Cotter End with excellent views back of Wensleydale

47

High Dyke

services were axed during the Beeching cuts and the line was heading for decay, but initiatives in the 1970's saw the old stations re-opened for Dales Rail trains and soon these stations were seeing regular services again. In the 1980's a campaign successfully saved the line from closure. The line is at present a viable concern and long may it remain so. It is certainly one of the most scenic routes in the country and on the days when the great steam trains are running, hundreds of enthusiasts from all over the country can be seen lining the route.

Along some of the wider parts of the path it's quite possible to imagine Lady Anne travelling in her horse-litter, accompanied by her servants and tenants, whilst on other sections the imagination is stretched to the limit. The view of Wild Boar Fell on your left with its rocky profile rising to 2,324ft is the same as the one that Lady Anne looked upon several centuries before us, likewise the cliff face of Mallerstang Edge which dominates the other side of the valley.

Whilst on the 'Highway' you will pass three groups of deserted buildings. The third set of ruins, known as High Hall, was once an inn providing accommodation and refreshments for travellers (GR 794957). Shortly after reaching this, the wall on your left drops down the fellside to the road, but your way is straight on towards Hell Gill

Bridge, hidden amongst a group of trees. The present bridge was built in 1820 to replace a much earlier packhorse bridge. Hell Gill Beck is in fact the youthful River Eden. Do pause to look over the bridge on the right side, as it is a steep sided ravine of some significance.

Local legend has it that a highwayman leapt over this gully on horseback to escape capture. The bridge marks the boundary between Yorkshire and Cumbria (traditionally Westmorland) and was once the extremity of the National Park. (If the gorge is followed downhill you will reach Hell Gill Force - an impressive sight when water is cascading over the edge or in winter when hung with icicles). Once over the bridge carry on along the 'Highway', which at this point is a lovely wide grassy plateau.

Whilst walking this stretch in early summer Frank and I disturbed two lapwings who were at pains to make sure that we didn't discover their nest. The infant river Eden has its source high up on Black Fell Moss away to your right; on the moss is a pillar which Lady Anne had erected to mark the

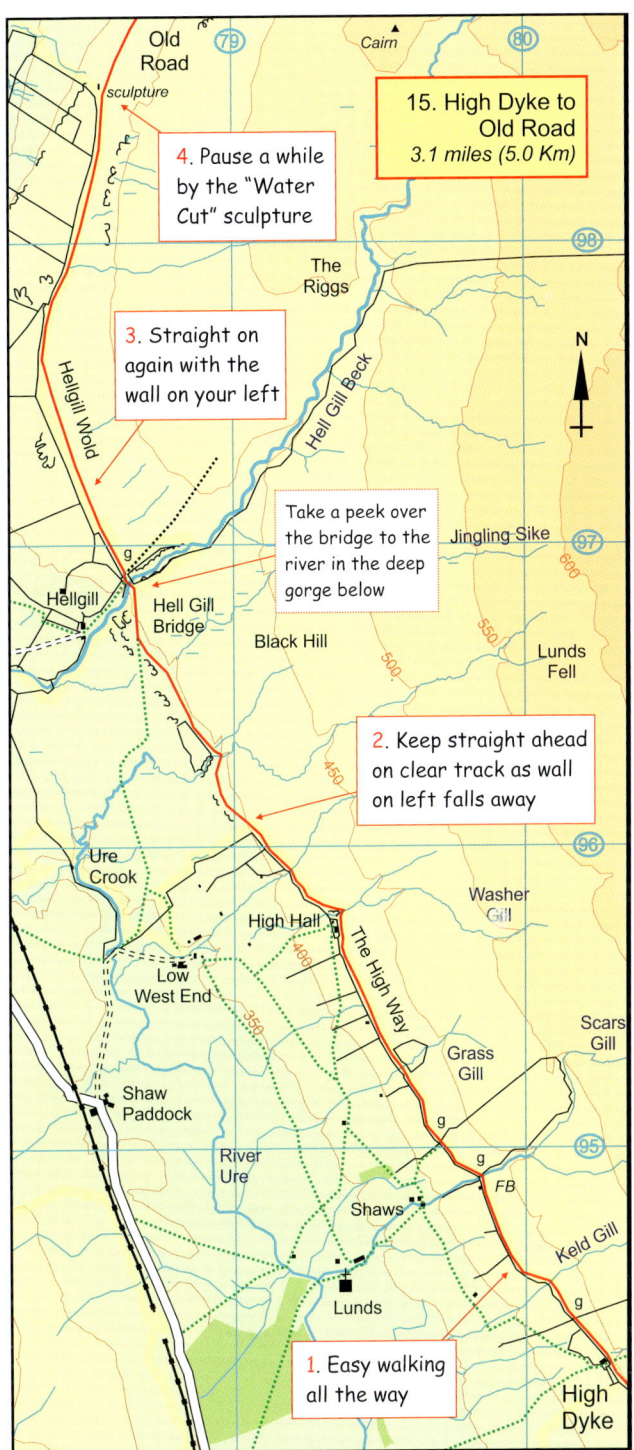

15. High Dyke to Old Road
3.1 miles (5.0 Km)

4. Pause a while by the "Water Cut" sculpture

3. Straight on again with the wall on your left

Take a peek over the bridge to the river in the deep gorge below

2. Keep straight ahead on clear track as wall on left falls away

1. Easy walking all the way

Water Cut by Mary Bourne

eastern boundary of her beloved Westmorland. The date of 1664 appears on the stone, together with that of 1890 when it was restored. Also on the pillar are the initials AP which stand for Anne Pembroke, Lady Anne's married name by her second husband. Repaired once more in 1953, the pillar stands as a constant reminder of a remarkable lady.

Eventually the 'Highway' starts to drop down to the road in the valley bottom. Here you will find a dramatic sculpture called "Water Cut" by Mary Bourne. This is one of a series of ten sculptures commissioned by East Cumbria Countryside Project and known as the Eden Benchmarks. It also provides a useful seat from which to view the sweeping landscape. As you descend wonderful views begin to unfold of the river Eden winding through Mallerstang with the

River Eden at Thrang Bridge

The Thrang Gate

North Pennines in the far distance. It is downhill now all the way to the road (at GR 783004) where a right turn here takes you towards the Thrang.

The word thrang means 'busy place', which would certainly have been the case when the drovers stopped here to water their cattle. Just before the buildings is a footpath on your left, which goes to Deep Gill; follow the track as it winds down to the river. Cross over the bridge and turn immediately right to follow the banks of the river Eden. On reaching a group of buildings, keep on the main track between farm buildings to a T-junction and a metalled road. Turn right here, and then almost immediately left across the field to go over a stone stile in the wall ahead. You are now back on the riverbank; follow this to a farm track and turn left to the hamlet of Shoregill.

Just across the river from here is the church of St. Mary's, adjacent to the slightly larger hamlet of Outhgill. The church was yet another building which Lady Anne restored in 1663 for a sum recorded as £46.15s. There are some of us who even remember this old currency! In addition she bought land near Sedbergh to provide money to maintain the church. In her usual fashion she had an inscription put on a stone over the porch door. The present one is a copy made to replace the original which was damaged:

THIS CHAPPLE OF MALLERSTANG AFTER IT HAD LAYNE RUNOUS AND DECAYED SOME 50 OR 60 YEARS WAS NEWE REPAYRED BY THE LADY ANNE CLIFFORD COUNTESSE DOWAGER OF PEMBROKE DORSETT AND MONTOGOMERY. IN THE YEAR 1663 WHO ALLSOE ENDOWED THE SAME WITH LANDS WHICH SHE PURCHASED IN CAUTLEY NEAR SEDBERG TO THE YEARLY VALUE OF ELEVEN POUNDS FOR EVER.

ISAIAH CHAP. 5,VER. 12. GODS NAME BE PRAISED.

Buried on the south side of the churchyard, in unmarked graves, lie the remains of many who died during the building of the Settle to Carlisle railway line which is just west of you. The hamlet of Outhgill once boasted a pub called the King's Head, which was for many years the main inn of the dale, unfortunately for our purposes the building was demolished in the 1840's. A stone rescued from the inn and dated 1665 can be seen above the loft door of an old barn at the south end of the village with a latin inscription which translated means "The inn keeper bids righteous folk to enter, but those who intend harm to go away".

Pendragon Castle

In the hamlet of Shoregill follow the walled track slightly uphill to a T-junction, turn right through a gate, then the right hand one of a pair of gates, followed by a stile between two gates. Follow the line of the directional arrows along a wall side, going through two fields and in the third go diagonally left over a stile. Turn right here to go through a gate ahead and then go diagonally left uphill to reach a further stile ahead. Keep on along the now obvious path, with a ruined barn over to your left, heading for a stone barn some distance ahead. At the end of this long field cross over a stone stile in the far left corner, turn right with a beck to reach a bridge over it. Carry on towards the barn (GR 780022), passing it on your right to reach a stile ahead. Once over this, go over the stile almost immediately on your right. The path here is indistinct but keep to the high ground within sight of the river.

Pendragon Castle is on the other side of the river beyond the trees. Soon the path drops down to a footbridge amongst the trees, and then follows the line of a fence towards a stable block. Behind this is a gate, which leads you onto a metalled road. A right turn will take you to a bridge over the Eden and to an excellent view of the castle.

Back to the present, and to the last few miles to Kirkby Stephen. Take the footpath on your left directly after crossing the bridge, which was originally built by Lady Anne in 1667. Go over a

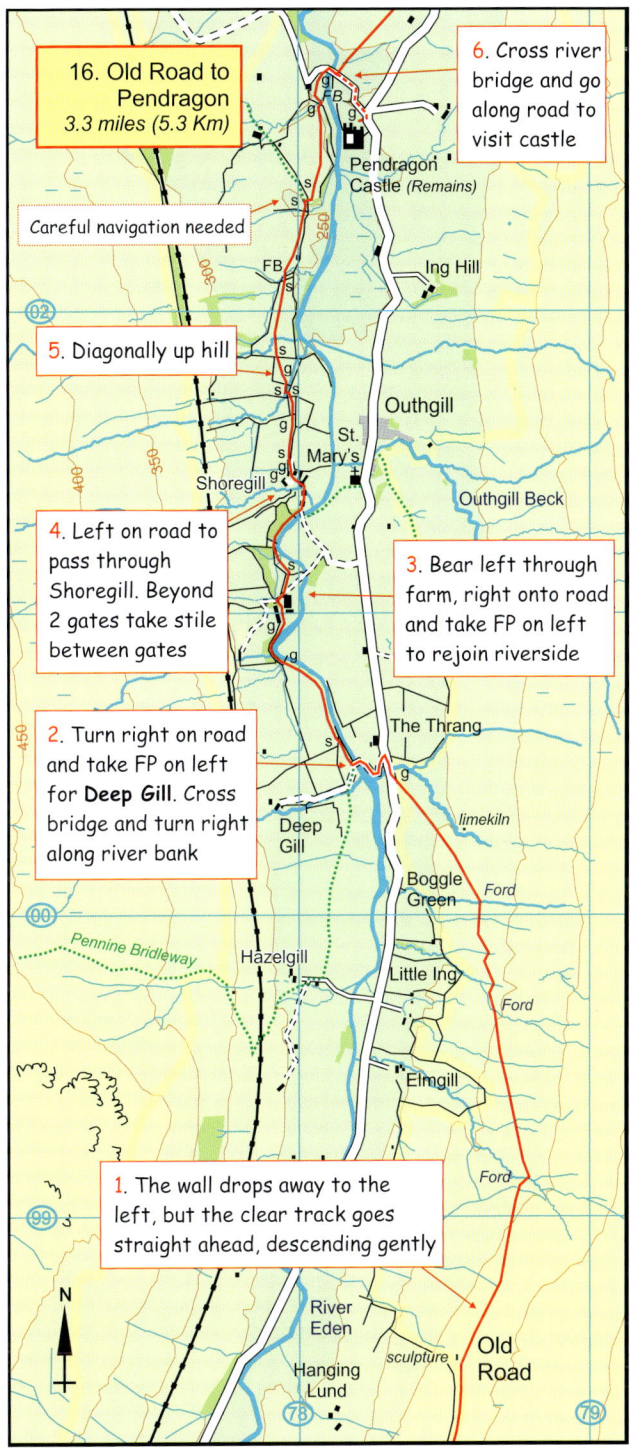

16. Old Road to Pendragon
3.3 miles (5.3 Km)

6. Cross river bridge and go along road to visit castle

Careful navigation needed

5. Diagonally up hill

4. Left on road to pass through Shoregill. Beyond 2 gates take stile between gates

3. Bear left through farm, right onto road and take FP on left to rejoin riverside

2. Turn right on road and take FP on left for **Deep Gill**. Cross bridge and turn right along river bank

1. The wall drops away to the left, but the clear track goes straight ahead, descending gently

Pendragon is now privately owned but the present owner has no objections to you having a look round provided that you remember to close the gate situated at the road junction. Local tradition has it that the castle was built by Uther Pendragon, father of the famous Arthur of the Round Table. In fact, the original wooden tower was built in the eleventh century and extended and strengthened by Robert Clifford about 1300. Unfortunately this was destroyed by the Scots in 1342, and was restored in stone by Roger Clifford some years later. This, in turn, was attacked in 1541 and laid in ruins until Lady Anne restored it in 1660. As usual, she left an inscription over the door:

> THIS PENDRAGON CASTLE WAS REPAYRED BY THE LADY ANNE CLIFFORD, COUNTESSE DOWAGER OF PEMBROKE, DORSET AND MONTGOMERIE, BARONESSE CLIFFORD, WESTMORLAND AND VESSIE HIGH SHERIFFESSE BY INHERITANCE OF THE COUNTY OF WESTMORLAND, AND LADY OF THE HONOUR OF SKIPTON-IN-CRAVEN IN THE YEAR 1660, SO AS SHE CAME TO LYE IN IT HERSELF FOR A LITTLE WHILE IN OCTOBER 1661, AFTER IT HAD LAYEN RUINOUS WITHOUT TIMBER OR ANY COVERING, EVER SINCE THE YEAR 1541.
>
> ISAIAH CHAP. 58, VER.12 GOD'S NAME BE PRASIED.

Pendragon was a very useful stopping point for Lady Anne on her route from Skipton through to her castles in the Eden Valley, and her diaries record one specific visit:

> "Soe I now kept Christmas here in this Pendragon Castle this yeare and this was the first time that I ever kept Christmas or any of my Ancestors before mee for 300 yeares before or more".

It is difficult now to imagine its former splendour or the many festivities which would accompany the Christmas period - all we are left with is a romantic ruin in a glorious setting.

stile ahead, keeping to the higher ground whilst walking towards a stone barn. After passing the barn on your right, go through the gateway on the right. Walk diagonally left towards a stile in a short section of stone wall ahead. Keeping in the same direction and aiming for a group of farm buildings, walk to the far right corner of the field where a gate leads out onto the Nateby road (GR 785033).

Turn left along the road until you reach a farm on your right known as Southwaite (signed to Nateby). Turn right here to reach the farm, and then left between the farm buildings to pass through the right-hand one of two wooden gates. Climb the hill, ignoring the metal gate ahead, and keep on uphill with a drystone wall on your left. Eventually you reach a metal gate ahead, go through here and turn immediately left following the indistinct path in a northerly direction across the field, keeping well to the right of a stone barn.

As you near the barn go diagonally right, over a stile ahead followed by a stream to reach a stone stile in the wall corner. Go over here

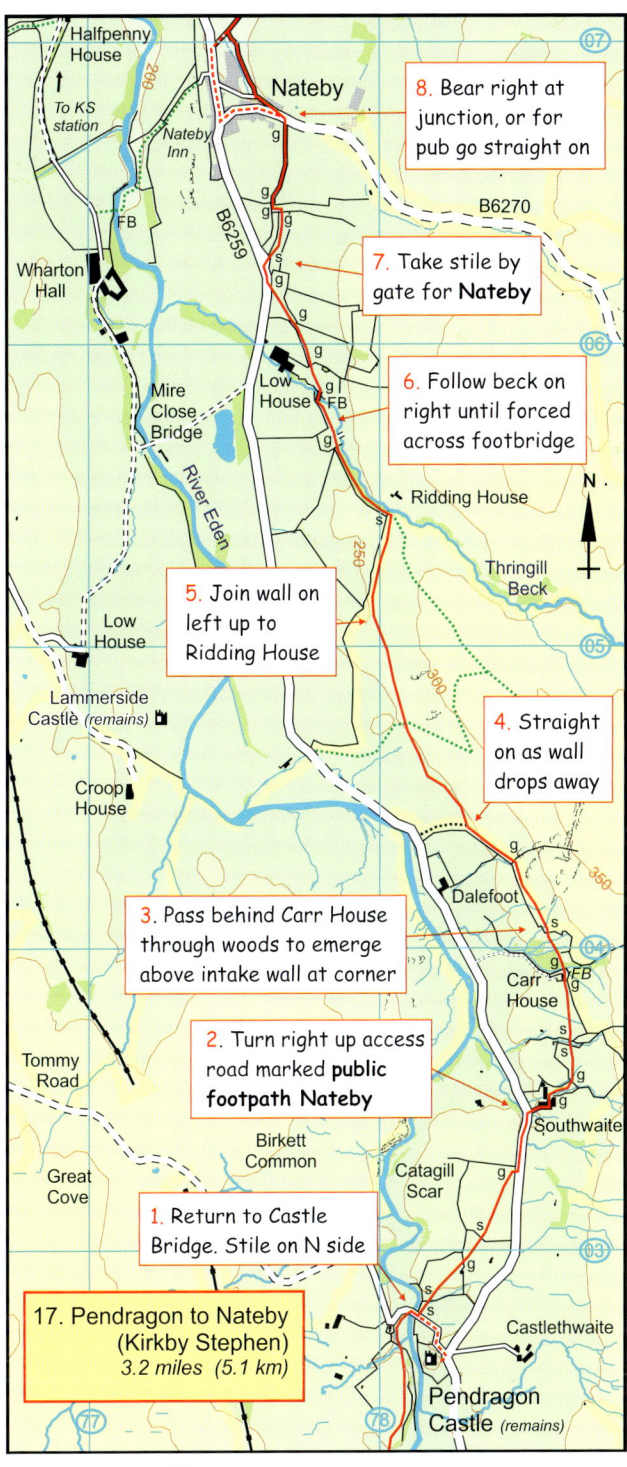

8. Bear right at junction, or for pub go straight on

7. Take stile by gate for **Nateby**

6. Follow beck on right until forced across footbridge

5. Join wall on left up to Ridding House

4. Straight on as wall drops away

3. Pass behind Carr House through woods to emerge above intake wall at corner

2. Turn right up access road marked **public footpath Nateby**

1. Return to Castle Bridge. Stile on N side

17. Pendragon to Nateby (Kirkby Stephen)
3.2 miles (5.1 km)

and keep straight on to cross the next field towards Carr House adjacent to a fence on your right (GR 786039).

Pass to the right of the house over a stile, footbridge and further stile and keep on through the trees, passing a ruined building on your right. Where an intake wall ahead comes down from the hillside on your right you will see a stone stile in the angle of the wall. Cross over this and follow the now obvious track, eventually coming out into an open area with the slopes of Great Bell on your right and the River Eden meandering away to your left.

On the far side of the river can be seen the remains of Lammerside Castle. Little is known about it, apart from the fact that it once belonged to the Wharton family, who own Wharton Hall about a mile further north.

Keep walking north, contouring around Great Bell and ignoring the footpath which drops down left to the road, beside a drystone wall. Follow the directional arrow straight ahead until you reach a good path coming in from the left. Go right here and follow this waymarked grassy path until, at a point where the ground starts to rise steeply (GR 780050) you reach a fork in the path. Take the left one, heading for a wall. This will take you all the way to the far left corner of the field and the ruins of Ridding House.

There is every amenity in Kirkby Stephen: shops, hotels, cafes and the Coast to Coast Chip Shop. Accommodation is no problem as the town hosts a youth hostel and a campsite as well as plentiful B & B establishments. It is a major stop-over for Coast to Coast walkers as well as being on the route of the Alternative Pennine Way, the Eden Way and The Yoredale Way - a veritable walkers crossroads.

Kirkby Stephen has always been a place of some importance, being on the main trading route from Wensleydale through the Eden Valley and over the North Pennines into Scotland. It was granted a charter in 1361 and has continued to hold a market every Monday. The cloisters between the church and the market square were built in 1810, originally to provide shelter for the market people and the churchgoers but they have also been utilized as a butter market.

The cobbled square marks the extremities of the bull baiting area which was used until early in the nineteenth century. In the eighteenth century, the town became famous for its woollen stockings which were knitted by both men and women throughout the area using local wool.

The parish church has many items of interest, including the famous Loki Stone - a Saxon carving of a bound devil. The tomb of Sir Richard Musgrave is here also, he who is reputed to have killed the last wild boar in the land-on Wild Boar Fell, of course. When his tomb was opened during some restoration work in the nineteenth century, a boar's tusk was found there. Also here is the tomb of Sir Thomas Wharton of Wharton Hall which you glimpsed on your way down from the slopes of Great Bell. Speaking of bells, Kirkby Stephen had a tradition of ringing the 'Taggy' bell at 8.00pm each evening as a curfew for children, otherwise the demon Taggy would pounce on them after dark.

On the felltops to the south-east of Kirkby Stephen rise nine cairns, known as Nine Standards Rigg. Their origin is unknown, although recent research has found references to them as early as the thirteenth century. Local legend has it that they were built to hoodwink the invading Scots into thinking that the English were there in great force. If the weather is clear they can be seen on your route out of Kirkby Stephen.

Go left here over a stile in the wall beside a gate and follow the ravine downhill to reach a gate. Wharton Hall is opposite on the other side of the valley. The Whartons were a powerful family in the area and they fortified the existing fourteenth century building and extended it further in the sixteenth.

After passing through the gate, keep straight on with a stream over to your right. At the end of the field turn right and go over a bridge and through the gate ahead. Turn left through the gate and keep straight on across the field to join a wall corner. Go through the gate ahead and keep on in the same direction with a wall on your left. Go through a further gate ahead and in this final field keep with the wall on your right until it swings away right. Keep straight on here to reach the Nateby Road.

Turn right along the road until you reach a lay-by on the right with a sign pointing to Nateby. Pass through the squeeze stile to the right of a gate and follow the fence on your left to a gate at the end of this field. Cross the next short section of field to a gate slightly to your left. This gives access to a walled lane leading you to the village of Nateby (GR 777067).

Turn left here and, if you're in need of refreshments, carry on to the main road where the Nateby Inn serves food and provides accommodation. Anyone wishing to camp at Kirkby Stephen and not in need

Kirkby Stephen

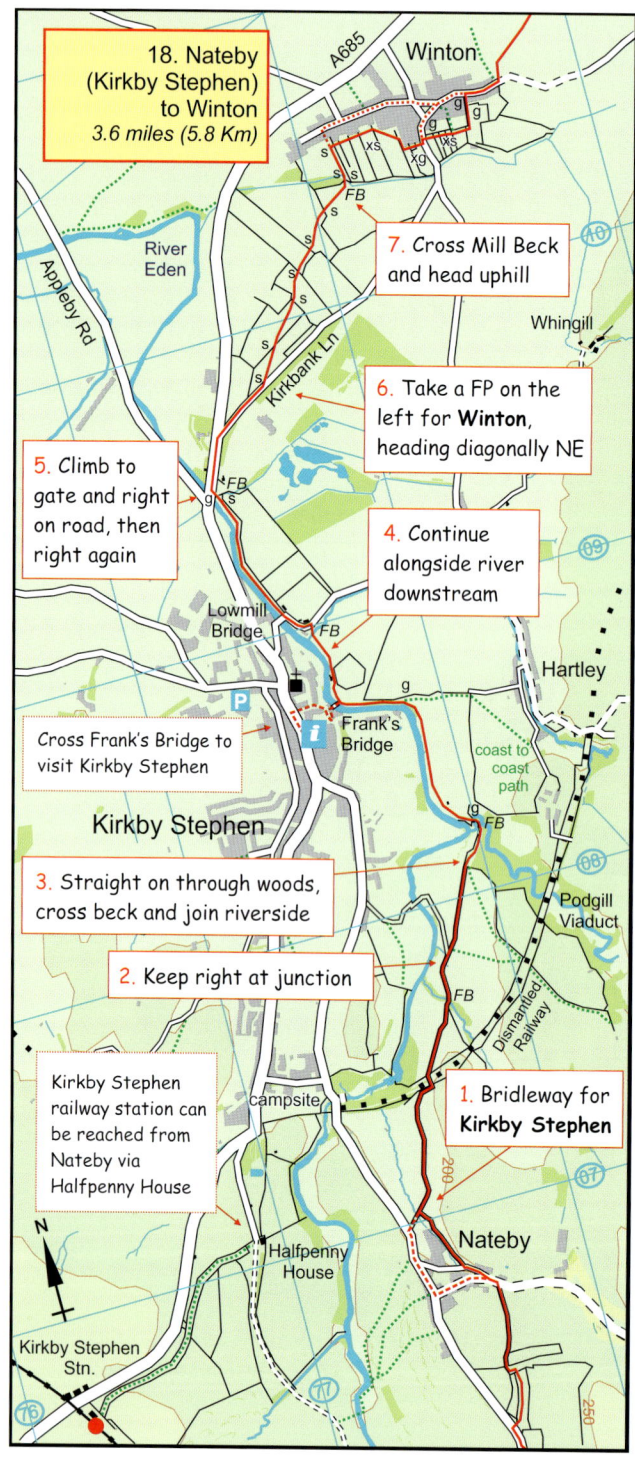

of provisions in the town would be well advised to walk to the main road as well, and follow it to the campsite: this lies a mile south of the town on the main Sedbergh road (GR 771076).

Otherwise cross the road and take a track which passes in front of a row of houses, on the far side of the stream. Shortly you will see a bridleway sign to Hartley on your right. Follow this walled lane and when you reach a junction of paths, turn right.

This is an excellent path which crosses over a disused railway and enters a wooded area. At a path junction take the right fork signed to Hartley and continue along the path as it crosses Ladthwaite Beck.

From here it is just a short stroll following the River Eden to Frank's Bridge, and so into Kirkby Stephen.

Once over Frank's Bridge take the steps on your right to reach the Market Square.

STAGE FIVE: Kirkby Stephen to Appleby

Distance: 16½ miles   *Total distance: 79¾ miles*

Ordnance Survey Maps 1:25,000 -

Explorer OL19 – Howgill Fells & Upper Eden Valley

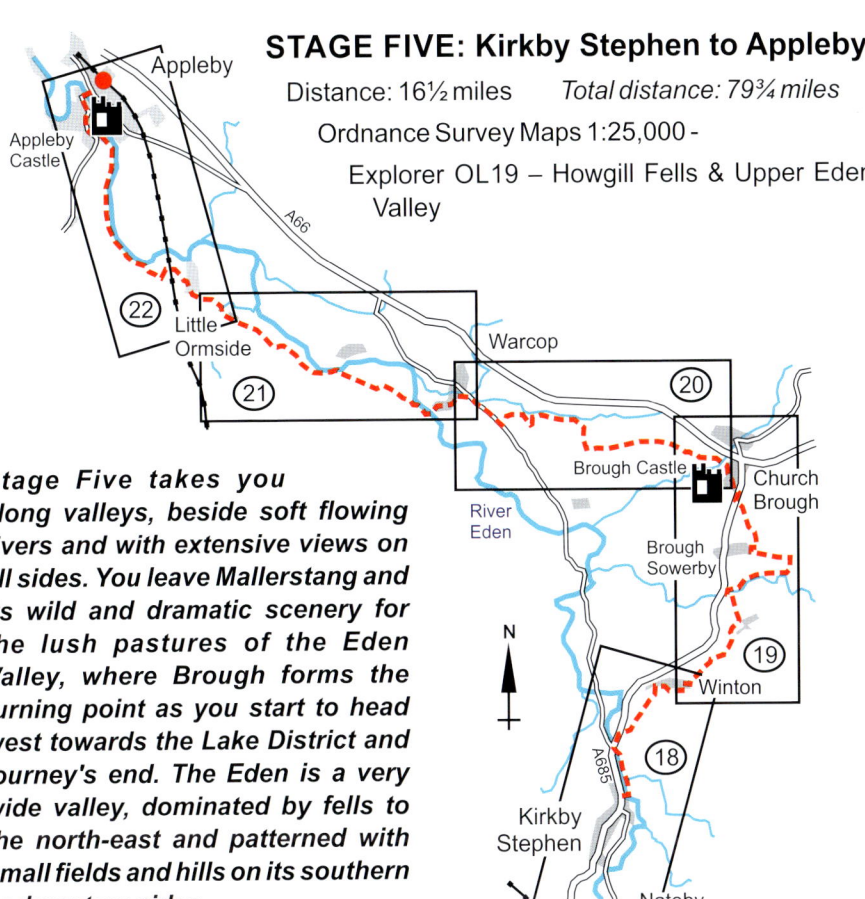

Stage Five takes you along valleys, beside soft flowing rivers and with extensive views on all sides. You leave Mallerstang and its wild and dramatic scenery for the lush pastures of the Eden Valley, where Brough forms the turning point as you start to head west towards the Lake District and journey's end. The Eden is a very wide valley, dominated by fells to the north-east and patterned with small fields and hills on its southern and western sides.

There is much of historical interest on today's walk, encompassing as it does the ruins of Brough Castle, Ormside 'Cross' and church, and finishing with Appleby and its splendid castle and churches. This is easy walking with only minor undulations and many spectacular views, so keep your camera handy.

Although travelling on foot, you may be able to identify with Lady Anne as she herself describes her rather more spectacular progress along this section in her diary: "Coming along in my Horselitter attended by my women servants in my coach, and my Menservants on horseback with a great many of the Gentrey and of my Neighbours and Tenants in both places, through Warcop, Bondgate and Appleby Bridge".

Leave Kirkby Stephen from the Market Place down a lane with the Cloisters (outside the Parish Church) on your left. A sign marked 'Frank's Bridge' points the way. This is also the route taken by Coast to Coast walkers out of Kirkby Stephen. A second sign to 'River Eden & Frank's Bridge' will soon be seen between houses on your left, and this directs you down to the riverbank.

Frank's Bridge is said to have been named after Francis Birbeck a local brewer, and was built in the seventeenth century. The bridge formed part of a corpse road and the large stones at the end of the bridge were used to rest the coffins on.

After crossing the bridge you leave the Coast to Coasters who bear right towards Hartley Fell and Nine Standards Rigg. Bear left following a sign to Lowmill and follow the riverbank downstream. Soon you reach a sports field where a glance over your right shoulder will reveal Nine Standards Rigg just visible on the skyline.

You will shortly go over a footbridge before reaching the road at Lowmill Bridge. Turn left along the road to reach a path on your right beside the bridge, which takes you back along the river bank: do not cross over the bridge. Follow this well marked riverside path to reach the road at New Bridge. Turn right here onto the A685, which has a good footpath, and take the first road off on your right which goes to Winton (GR 775097). You will pass Eden Place on your right, home to some exotic birds which may be seen on occasions flying in the area. It also has a fascinating pets' graveyard in the front garden - who Dandy, Peter, Rust, Jack, Thistle and Rock were we will never know, but it gives you something to ponder on during the miles ahead.

Take the footpath just ahead of you on the left, and marked to Winton. Go diagonally right in a north-easterly direction across the field to a stile in the fence ahead, carrying on in the same direction across the next two fields. In the third field follow the hedge right to a stile. In the fourth one, whilst keeping the same general direction, aim for the corner of the fence ahead identified by a telegraph pole. At the corner carry on ahead with the fence on your right, to reach a stile in the corner of the field. Cross the next field, go over Mill Beck and follow the paved trod uphill to reach the village of Winton.

Shortly before you reach the road you meet a gate, turn right in front of it over a stone stile which will take you behind the village. This will enable you to have a good look at the villagers' gardens. (If you prefer looking at their front gardens, then carry straight on to the road and turn right to walk through the village.)

The footpath behind the houses takes you through several gates and stiles in the same general direction, until you gain access to a large field with farm buildings ahead. Bear diagonally right here to reach a stile in the stone wall ahead, to the right of a metal gate. A left turn on the track here will take you to Winton village and the Bay Horse Inn which serves food and also provides accommodation. Otherwise follow the directional arrow to the right here and then immediately left over a stile and carry on behind the gardens to reach a tarmac road. Turn left here and then almost immediately right, and carry on past the rest of the village gardens. Eventually the stone wall on your left comes to an end and you must follow it round to the left, following a directional arrow to walk alongside a beautiful building built in the local red sandstone. You will emerge on the village street to meet up with your fellow walkers who have taken the alternative route.

Turn right here and as the road begins to rise, a footpath appears on your left to Kaber. Cross this field diagonally right to a wall corner and follow the wall round to the right. At the end of this long field, climb the stile beside the gate in the middle of the fence ahead of you. In front of you rise the hills of Stainmore Common and to the left the Warcop Fells. These act as a T-Junction with the A66 running beneath them and mark the end of the valley of Mallerstang and the start of the lovely Eden Valley.

In the same direction, cross the next field and go over the stile ahead of you, then turn immediately left along a hedge side to cross Sandwath Sike (GR 792110). Turn right and follow the sike and then a hedge on your right which soon bends left and then right, to reach a stile beside a gate. The houses of Kaber should now be in view. Go over the stile and follow the hedge on your left to reach a gate and stile ahead of you, which give access to a short section of track and so onto the road.

Turn right on the road towards Kaber, 'Eden's Best Kept Hamlet' according to a roadsign. Take the footpath on your left marked to 'Belah Bridge', immediately after passing the unclassified Popping Lane on your left, and just before the Kaber roadsign.

After going through the gate, in a few yards cross a stone slab over the tiny stream on your left and follow a wall to a footbridge over Popping Beck. Cross the corner of the next field and go over a further stile before crossing a marshy patch of ground. Climb left up the hill ahead in a northerly direction and

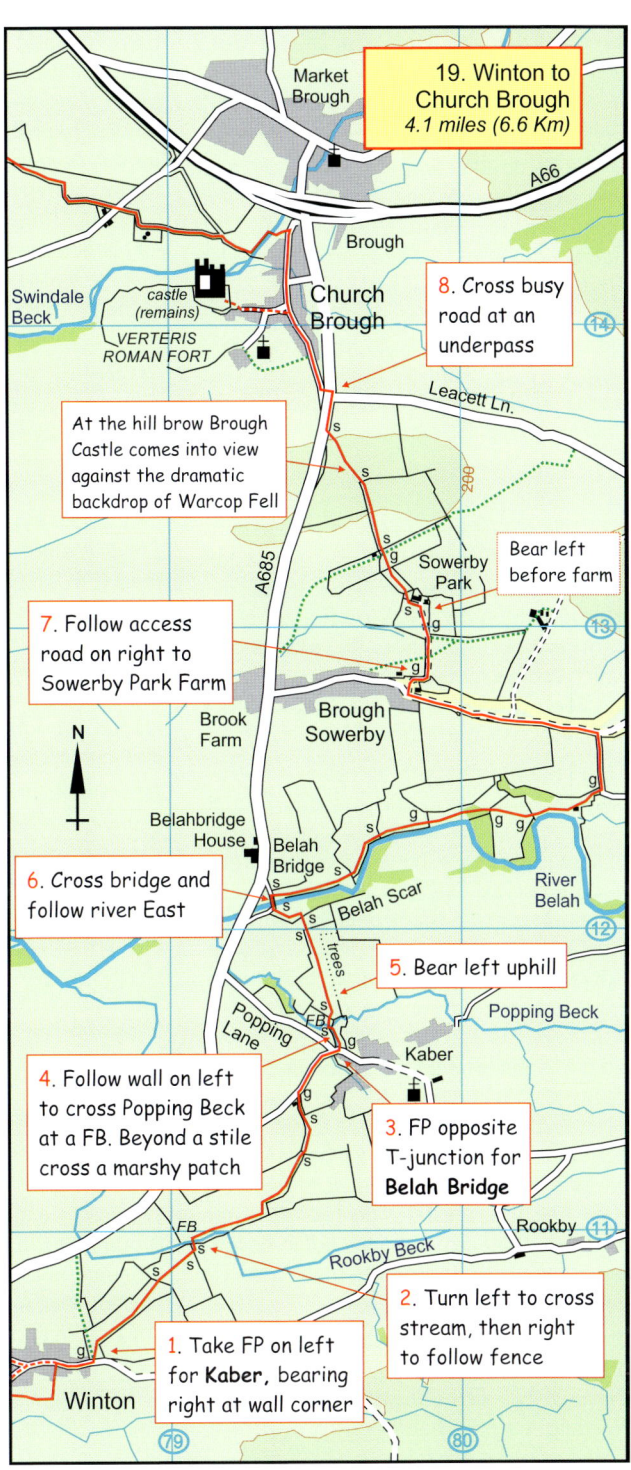

eventually you will have a line of trees either side of you. Keep on to reach a stile in the far left corner of the field (GR794120).

In the same direction cross the next field and cross the stile ahead before dropping down towards Belah Bridge. Cross the bridge and go immediately right over a stile along the northern side of the river. Belah Scar will soon become visible on the other side of the river, with its lovely red cliffs made up of Penrith Sandstone. This becomes the main building material the nearer you get to Carlisle.

After approximately half a mile the river turns to the right and your way lies straight ahead across the next field to a metal gate. Once through this follow the river again until you see a stone barn which is built into the side of the hill. Pass on the left of the barn and climb the track towards a gate which soon becomes visible in the corner of the field. This leads out onto a good track coming from Bloan Farm (GR 805124).

Turn left onto the track to reach a narrow road and turn left again towards Brough Sowerby. To your right are excellent views of Musgrave Fell with the quarry beneath it and further on, Warcop and Burton Fells, culminating in the unmistakeable shape of Roman Fell. As you approach Brough Sowerby, after approximately half a mile, there is a cleared area on your right; from here lovely views can be enjoyed of Wild Boar Fell in all its splendour, dominating the valley of Mallerstang. As you reach the houses of the village the road curves to the right and a footpath sign will be seen also on the right. Follow this track to Sowerby Park Farm. At the farm do not follow the track into the yard, but pass left in front of the garden boundary wall to reach a stile in the farm wall, well waymarked.

Cross diagonally left through the old orchard and keep straight ahead through the next two fields towards an old barn. Keeping the barn and hedge on your left,

carry on uphill to a final stile in the top left corner of the field. Go over here and carry on in a north-westerly direction over the brow of the hill. This is a dramatic moment as the dominating bulk of Brough Castle towers above the scene, standing sentinel over the Eden Valley. At this point we must say farewell to Mallerstang and its haunting beauty, and also to Wild Boar Fell which is etched on the skyline behind.

Drop down left to a squeeze stile in the wall to meet the A685. Follow the grass verge right, until you reach a road off to your right. Go right here and then immediately left to reach an underpass which takes you beneath the A685. Turn right out of here and follow the road into Church Brough. Those wishing to visit the ruins of the castle must turn left on reaching the centre of the village, where signposted. A farm beside the castle has a teashop and ice cream parlour, whilst other amenities are available only a quarter of a mile away at Market Brough, including accommodation for those ending the day here.

From the centre of Church Brough carry on along the road over the road bridge and past the school to reach a gate on your left. Go through here and follow the concrete path down to the river. Go over the bridge and turn left, go over a stile to enter a nature reserve, following a path beside the river. At the field corner drop down through the trees and over a stile to reach a good track. Turn right here, (unless you fancy a paddle!) and follow the track which is adjacent to the sports field. At the end of the sports field leave the track, going left along an enclosed lane beside a gate.

There are excellent views along here of Brough Castle in its prominent position at the head of the valley. The reasons for its position become obvious, standing as it does on raised ground with the river here on its northern side and a moat on its other side made it easy to defend.

Follow the track until it emerges onto

Brough Castle

Brough lies at the foot of the pass across the Pennines known as Stainmore and has been a place of some importance for this very reason. The Romans built a military road from York to Carlisle which went through Brough and built a fort on the mound on which now stand the ruins of Brough Castle. A thousand years after the Romans, the Normans built their castle on the same site. This was destroyed by the invading Scots in 1174 and rebuilt towards the end of the century. Robert, the first of the Northern Cliffords, built the Round Tower in 1300 and the main block was built fifty years later by his grandson Rodger. The whole was destroyed by fire in the sixteenth century and it was left in neglect until the next century when Lady Anne set to work.

The village church dates from 1150 and amongst other features has a 'leper's squint' (a slit in the wall) to enable members of the congregation excluded from the service for any reason (such as infectious diseases) to see the altar. You will see another example of this at the church at Great Ormside, not many miles from Appleby. Both church and castle lie in Church Brough, whilst Market Brough on the other side of the main A66 has all the modern amenities. This was the centre of trade from as early as 1330, when a charter for a weekly market was granted. One of the ancient customs unique to Brough was the burning of a holly bush on Twelfth Night.

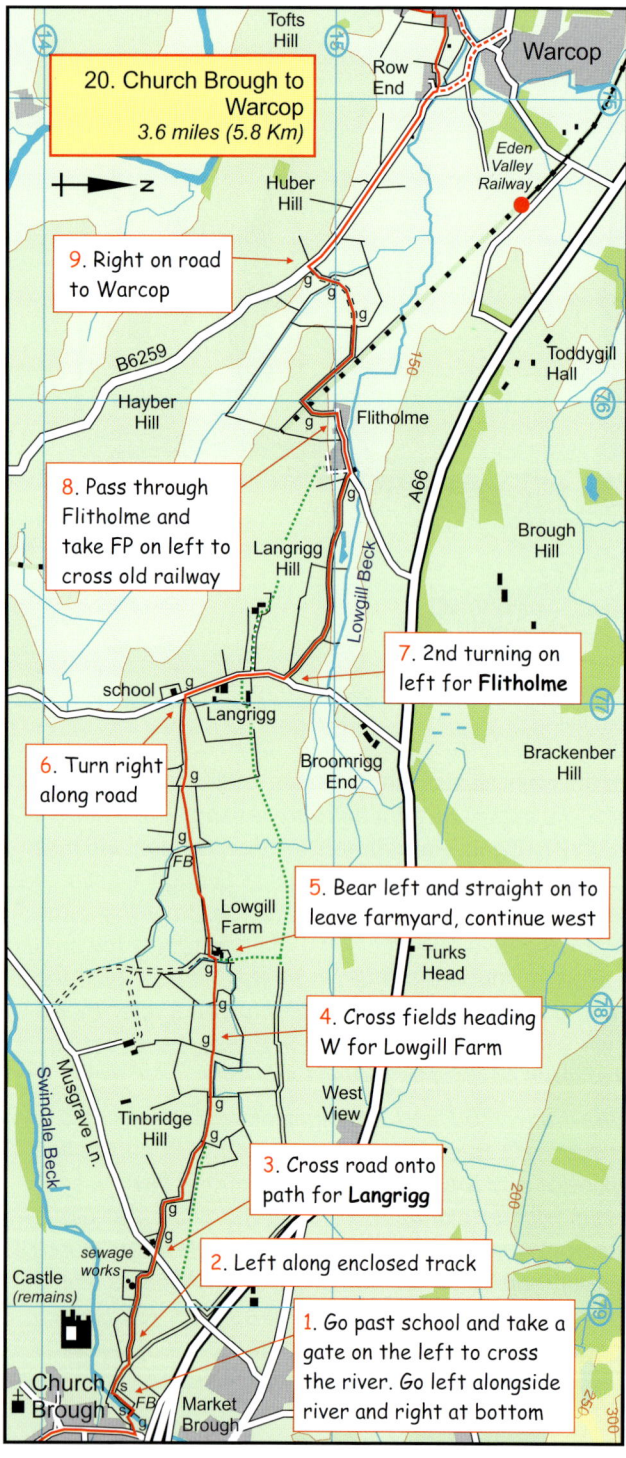

Musgrave Lane, and go straight over the road and take the track opposite signed to Langrigg. Soon the track bears right, and you need to take the right one of two gates. Shortly the track opens out into a field; here you need to turn left, keeping the wall and fence on your left to pass through a gate at the end of the field.

Over to your right on a rocky outcrop amongst the trees is the Fox Tower, built in 1775 for John Metcalfe Carleton, owner of nearby Hellbeck Hall. The tower included two circular rooms giving far reaching views of the Howgills and the Lake District. Also on one side was a smaller but taller tower complete with spiral staircase. Local lore has it that the tower was built by the owner to enable him to watch the hunt after he had suffered an injury. Whether true or not, it makes a nice story.

Keeping the same direction, pass through a gate at the end of the following field. Keep straight on, heading for Lowgill farm, and going through a gate in the fence ahead of you. In spring these lowland fields are full of lambs, and their uninhibited antics lift the spirits as well as making a very pretty picture. In the same westerly direction cross the next field to a gate at a fence corner. Once through this, keep straight ahead to Lowgill Farm (GR 778146).

Go through the gate, passing the farmhouse on your right, keeping straight on along a vague cart track between 2 short rows of hedging to cross this field. At the end of the field go slightly left to reach a bridge. Then aim diagonally left across the next field to reach a gate in the far left corner (or you may prefer to go round the edge of the field). Follow the now obvious track due west to reach the road at Langrigg. Just across the road is the old school, now converted to a house, where an inscription can be seen on the gable end.

Langrigg

Turn right here and follow the road for approximately a quarter of a mile as it rises to contour Langrigg Hill. Ignore the first footpath on your left to Flitholme and take the second one, a bridleway which is reached at the crest of the hill. This is a good path, approximately half a mile long which takes you all the way to Flitholme with no route finding problems. You may well hear artillery fire along this stretch, as the Warcop Army Training Centre is just across the fields on your right and some of the buildings and the lookout post can be seen clearly.

There is a good public footpath along the top of the fells here which would make an excellent alternative high level route from Brough to Appleby. Unfortunately, access is limited to the times when the army is not in training, and so it is not suitable for our purposes. Certainly the large number of used shells encountered on the ground would be enough to deter all but the most determined of travellers. It may be possible one day to offer an alternative route over these wonderfully majestic fells. In the meantime however we must enjoy the pleasures of the valley and appreciate the beauty of these fells from a distance.

Turn left on reaching the road and go through the hamlet of Flitholme until you come to a footpath sign on your left at the end of the tarmac. Follow the path as it rises to a bridge over the disused railway track and then turns right to run alongside the track for approximately 200 yards. Remnants of a possible railway crossing are still in evidence and just after passing the ruined building, the path makes a left turn and eventually gives access into a large field. Keep straight on to reach a track, turn left along here to reach the B6259 (GR 755149).

A right turn here will bring you after

Warcop Old Bridge

approximately half a mile to Row End Farm, situated directly after the Warcop road sign. (Note that at this point Warcop village centre can be reached just ahead by remaining on the road and going right at the junction.) After passing the farm the road curves to the right (note the Andy Goldsworthy sculpture on your right) and here you will see a footpath sign directly ahead of you. Pass through the wooden gate and walk due east with a farm cottage on your left.

Ignore the farm track as it curves away to your left, but keep straight ahead to go through a small metal gate in the stone wall in front. The gate is situated beyond some rough ground and may take some searching out in high summer if the ground has not been cleared. Keep a stone wall on your right to the end of this field, and pass through the stile ahead of you to reach a group of houses.

Follow the waymark straight on to a road. Turn left here amongst a group of houses and, at the end of the road, turn right and then left to go alongside a hedge to reach a kissing gate. Keep the fence and

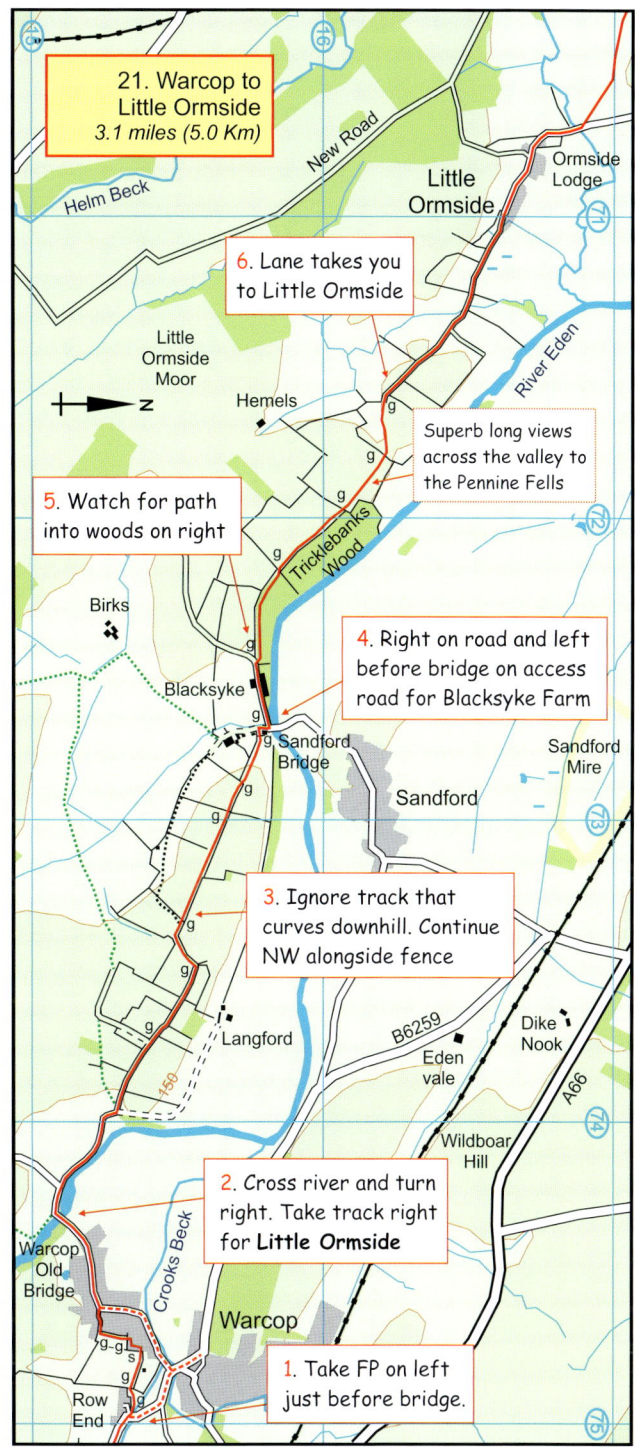

hedge on your right to reach a further gate at the far end of the field. Go right here onto a track to join a road. Ignore the road which rises on your left and carry straight on to a T-junction. Turn left here through the village to eventually drop down to Warcop Old Bridge.

In February the high banks on either side are carpeted with snowdrops, making a delightfully welcome sight in what can sometimes be a dreary month. The Eden is quite wide at this point as it flows merrily under Warcop Bridge - it has grown and matured mightily since its birth high up on the fellside above Mallerstang. Once over the bridge, the road makes a right turn alongside the riverbank before turning left. At this point (GR 742151) take the track straight ahead signed to 'Little Ormside'.

Keep to the main concrete farm track. The track starts to rise and you reach a bridleway going off left. Follow this left, ignoring the now tarmac track which carries straight on towards Langford Farm. Keep on the bridleway, climbing uphill until at GR 737154 the track curves away to the left, but your route is straight ahead on a green path between hedges. Keep straight on through a gate across your path. Follow this twin-wheeled track, with a hedge either side, as it swings left through another gate. Keep with a hedge on your right, turning right with it and very soon the track curves away left to go down hill. Leave it and go straight on through another gate in the fence ahead.

Keep to the high ground and with the hedge still on your right, pass through a series of fields until the buildings of Blacksyke come into view. As the ground starts to fall away you will reach a wooden gate straight ahead. Pass through this and drop down the hill with the hedge now on your left to reach a gate giving access to a track. Turn right past a pebble-dashed house to reach the riverbank once more. (Do not cross over the river unless you are in need of refreshments; just under a quarter of a mile over the bridge is the village of Sandford, with a pub.)

Otherwise turn left to follow the river to reach Blacksyke Farm. Pass through the middle of the farm buildings and take the path through a gate diagonally right to enter woodland. Ignore the farm track as it curves away to the left (GR 725158). The path rises uphill with Tricklebanks Wood on your right. Pass through a gate at the top, and follow the path round to the right as it follows the perimeter of the wood.

As the woodland ends, glorious views unfold of the lush Eden Valley nestling beneath the Murton and Warcop Fells. It is such a wide valley that one never gets that closed-in feeling and consequently the views are so much more extensive. Long Fell and Roman Fell are close to hand on your right and the rest of the range is clearly visible as far as the biggest of them all, Cross Fell. Westwards in the far distance on a clear day can be seen the Lakeland Fells, with the Howgill Fells further to their left.

Go through a metal gate at the end of this field and on through a further gate. Follow the twin tracks as they contour round the hill ahead to reach a gate which gives access onto a lane. After approximately half a mile Ormside Lodge is reached, in the front garden of which stands a magnificent cedar tree said to have been brought back from the Lebanon by General Whitehead. He supposedly grew the sapling in his hat during the long sea voyage to England and shared his daily ration of water with it. Carry straight on past the Lodge, disregarding the track off to the left unless you are looking for a campsite.

A little over a mile from here along this track known as Mill Lane, lies the award winning Wild Rose Caravan Park, named for the roses which grow in the hedgerows. To reach the camp site at GR 698167 follow Mill Lane as it climbs up through the wood to eventually drop down to Ormside Mill. Take the stepping stones across the

Great Ormside

stream and follow the lane left under the railway bridge and so to the site. The route out to Great Ormside the following day is easy enough, turning left out of the site and then right at the T-junction and so to the village of Ormside to rejoin the route.

Carry on along the metalled track until it becomes a road passing over Helm Beck. Almost immediately a footpath sign will be seen on your left. Take this diagonally right across the field in line with the telegraph poles to a stile in the hedge ahead of you. Once over this follow the poles again to a further stile and then bear left to a metal gate in the fence ahead. A further two stiles and then another one beside a metal gate will take you into the last field, where you need to bear left to a final metal gate which takes you out onto the road. A right turn will bring you to Great Ormside, passing a long white building known as Bromley Green. It was built on a plinth of boulders and the date 1687 can be seen on one of the door lintels; little seems to have changed in the intervening centuries apart from a lick of paint. Ignore the left fork in the road to come to a junction. On the other side of the road and left of a Victorian post box will be seen a footpath sign which directs you between two gardens.

However, if you have time on your hands, turn right here to visit the parish church of St. James which has much of interest. Along this road on the side of a building can be seen an old AA sign, sporting what looks suspiciously like bullet holes. The sign gives the mileage to Appleby and Soulby, but also the useful tip that London is only 273 miles away. These enamelled signs were erected by the AA between the wars with the advent of mass motoring and are now collectors' items.

As you approach the church a large sycamore tree will be seen growing from the centre of an ancient but impressive arrangement of steps. This was the site of the old preaching cross which can be found by the church path. The cross was the focal point for the local cheese and butter market, held regularly until recent times. The parish church is built on a part natural, part artificial mound. This has yielded some important archaeological finds, including an Anglo Saxon cup which is recognised as being one of the best pieces of metalwork from the Dark Ages. The Ormside Cup was found in the churchyard in 1823 and is at present in the Yorkshire Museum. Other items discovered in the mound include a hoard of brass and pewter and a Viking sword.

The tower and nave of the church are of Norman origin, while the oak roof and much of the furnishings are seventeenth century. The hagioscope or 'leper's squint' mentioned earlier can be seen to the left of the altar. This area is now enclosed by the vestry which has a beacon window giving views of the ford across the River Eden. During the Border raids a lamp was left burning in the window to guide those travellers heading for the church in search of sanctuary. On an early reconnaisance of this area my colleagues and I walked many miles in the confident expectation of being able to cross the river here only to discover the hoped-for bridge did not exist. As for the idea of fording the river, 'swim' would be a better word. As you leave the churchyard, Ormside Hall can be seen on the left with its fourteenth century pele tower; originally on three floors and probably battlemented, it is now a private residence.

If you have taken time to visit the church you need only retrace your steps as far as the site of the village cross; a right turn here along a farm track will take you to the path under the railway.

For those of you back at the T-junction - take the path indicated, between two gardens, and go over a wooden stile which gives access into a large field. Cross the field passing through a gate followed by a further one to reach a track. Turn left here and keep left uphill to go under the railway, rejoining your fellow walkers at this point, where a concrete ladder-stile ahead takes you into a field.

Keeping the hedge on your left, follow the path round to the left along a very wide path bounded by hedges. Go through the gateway at the end, turn right here and walk downhill to a stile ahead which takes you into a wooded area with a deeply cut stream on your left.

Descend to the wooden footbridge over Jeremy Gill and follow the fence up to the right until a stile in the fence is reached. Carry on over the stile and follow the obvious path uphill, with mixed woodland on your right which falls away down to the river Eden, flowing wide and deep below you. The path stays to the high ground for approximately quarter of a mile; the distinctive shape of Roman Fell may be seen etched sharply on the skyline to your right. Eventually a waymark (GR 691177) points the way downwards to the riverbank. At this point in Spring the ground is covered in wild garlic, its strong perfume pervading the air.

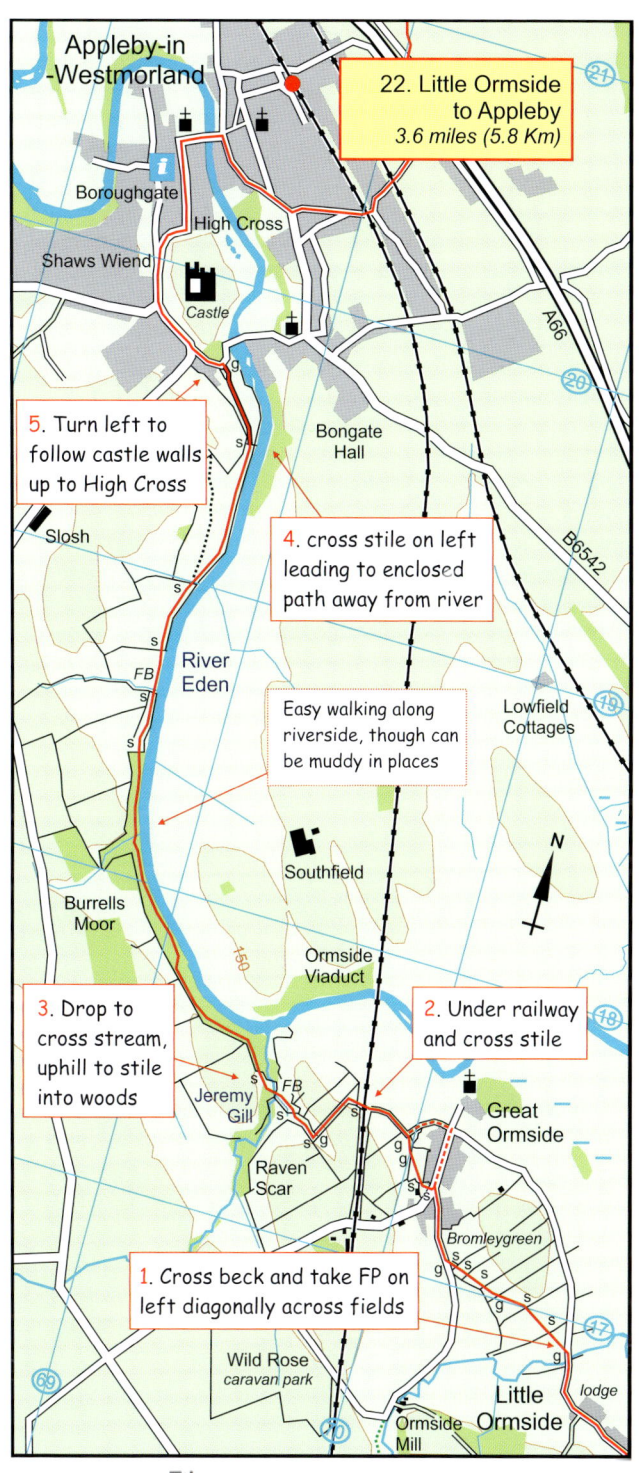

22. Little Ormside to Appleby
3.6 miles (5.8 Km)

From here it is very pleasant and easy walking alongside the Eden as it glides gently along all the way to Appleby - a distance of approximately 1¼ miles. The river makes a delightful companion as you weave your way amongst the trees, the countryside is green and lush and the soft rolling hills backed by the majestic fells provide a fitting end to a perfect day's walking.

Eventually a boundary fence will be seen straight ahead, and a stile on the right - this is for fishermen only. Our route lies over the stile in the left corner of this field (GR 688195). This gives access to a fenced path which ends in a kissing gate. To your right is the ford across the Eden, with the modern Jubilee Bridge beside it and Bongate Mill on the opposite bank. The original bridge was destroyed by floods in 1968 and the new higher bridge replaced it in 1970. Upstream is a weir where salmon can be seen leaping in the autumn. To the left is Castle Bank and the last part of today's walk. Turn left and follow the castle walls uphill and round to the right, ignoring all roads off to the left. With the castle walls still on your right, carry on to the main entrance and the top of the main street in Appleby known as Boroughgate.

I must admit to gasping with sheer delight when I first saw this view on a cold but bright day in February, when the lack of cars allowed the full beauty of the scene to be appreciated. The Castle Keep dominates the main street as one gazes down a wide tree-lined street with the Moot Hall part way down, whilst facing you at the bottom is the Parish church of St. Lawrence fronted by the Cloister arches. Two tall Regency columns standing on much earlier bases can be seen, one before the castle and the other outside the church, each topped by an ornate sundial. These proudly stand sentinel at each end of the main street and are still called the High and Low Crosses.

Appleby has all amenities and makes a

Boroughgate, Appleby

delightful stop-over with one reservation: for one week in the year it is the centre for what is reputed to be the largest horse fair of its kind in the world. Travelling people and horse-traders gather from about seven days prior to the sale (which is held on the second Wednesday in June) and the town of Appleby is bursting at the seams.

It is here that our problem lies, because accommodation both in and out of the town is booked as far ahead as three years in advance and so I strongly recommend that you avoid this one week in the year when planning your walk - unless you intend sleeping under a hedge! The fair is said to have existed under the protection of a charter given by James II in 1685 and takes place on Fair Hill (formerly Gallows Hill) which will be passed on the next stage.

The travelling people meet old friends and traders and set up all manner of stalls, while horse-traders conduct their business daily and can be seen washing their horses in the River Eden by the main bridge.

There is much to see in Appleby and, wherever you go, you will come across references to Lady Anne who played such an important role in the life of the town. The castle itself was on the site of a motte and bailey built before 1100 and replaced soon after with the keep, later called Caesar's Tower. This suffered under the hands of the Scots and later the Parliamentarians and was left a ruin until Lady Anne embarked on her restoration work. Unfortunately there is no inscription left at Appleby to record the fact as the original has perished, but we have an entry in one of her famous diaries:

> "...and in this year, 1651, the 21rst of April, I helped to lay the foundation stone of the middle wall of the great tower, called Caesar's Tower, to the end it might be repaired again and made habitable, if it pleased God, Isaiah LV111 12, which tower was wholly finished and covered with lead the latter end of July, 1653".

One of the main attractions of the castle was The Great Picture of the Clifford family, a triptych measuring approximately eighteen and a half by nine feet, which had been restored to its original home in the Great Hall.

The left hand panel depicts Lady Anne at fifteen years old in the year that her father died and when she expected to inherit her estates; the right hand panel shows her in 1646 when she finally did regain her estates and is the only portion to be painted from life. The central portion shows her parents and her two brothers who died in childhood. The triptych is no longer at the castle but can be seen at Abbot Hall Gallery & Museum at Kendal.

Amongst her other works, Lady Anne had a series of almshouses built which became known as the Hospital of St. Anne. Situated half-way up the main street, they provide a tranquil and other-worldly oasis, built in a

Washing horses at Appleby

Almshouses, Appleby

quadrangle shape around a courtyard with a central fountain. The public are allowed into the square which represents a delightful step back into the past, remaining as it was when first built. For the Chapel opening hours see a notice in the porch; this simple and dignified place of worship is well worth a visit, housing as it does a studded oak box given to the ladies by Lady Anne. The walls are adorned with biblical texts as well as the set of rules to which all the ladies must adhere. One states that the doors are to be locked at 9.30pm every day. On my visit, I was graciously shown round by one of the ladies, who explained how each tenant is responsible for tending the little flower beds outside each door; indeed, the whole is meticulously maintained, in keeping with Lady Anne's detailed instructions.

The parish church of St. Lawrence was also repaired by Lady Anne, and a vault built in the north-east corner "for myself to be buried in, if it please God"- its position is marked by a large stone slab with iron rings. Above it is a black marble tomb encrusted with shields illustrating the Clifford lineage. When the vault was opened in 1884 her body was discovered, in accordance with her will, encased in lead on a rough stone bench and with a brass inscription on her breast. Close by is the tomb erected by Lady Anne in 1617 to her mother Margaret, Countess of Cumberland. This elaborate tomb is topped with an alabaster effigy whose head rests on a cushion with a lamb at her feet. In true fashion Lady Anne left her mark on a beam in the Lady Chapel with the inscription "ANN COVNTESS OF PEMBROKE IN ANO 1655 REPAIRED ALL THIS BVILDING". Of further interest is the large organ given to the Corporation of Appleby in 1683 and thought to be one of the oldest working organs left in England. The Coronation pew is ornately carved and lined in a plush red fabric. It consists of three rows of seats for Councillors and one for the Mayor and is still used by the Council on special occasions.

There is much more to discover and a booklet at the back of the church, 'The Parish Churches of Appleby' by Martin Holmes is very informative. The church of Bondgate was another of Lady Anne's projects - I could go on, but you will find excellent information about the delights of Appleby and the surrounding area by paying a visit to the Moot Hall which houses the local information centre. The oak panelled upper storey is still used by the Town Mayor and Town Council for their meetings. One final point of interest: until recent times a bull ring, last used for bull-baiting in 1812, could be found in the ground close to the Low Cross. This however had to be removed for safety reasons - which explains why a colleague and I had no success, one moonlit February night, in finding it! The bull ring is now on display at the Moot Hall.

STAGE SIX: Appleby to Penrith

Distance: 19¾ miles   Total distance: 99½ miles

Ordnance Survey Maps 1:25,000 -

OL 19 – Howgill Fells & Upper Eden Valley;
OL 5 – The English Lakes North-Eastern Area

Stage Six follows a low level route with superb views of the North Pennine hills. Delightful villages are visited which have changed little for generations, and are a joy to the eye with their buildings of soft red sandstone. The ancient ruins of Brougham Hall and its accompanying craft centre and cafe are passed before the culmination of the walk, when the magnificent ruins of Brougham Castle are reached. All then that is left is a short stretch of riverside walking before you arrive at the outskirts of Penrith and the end of Lady Anne's Way is in sight.

(This stage could be split up at Temple Sowerby, which is off-route just beyond Ousenstand Bridge.)

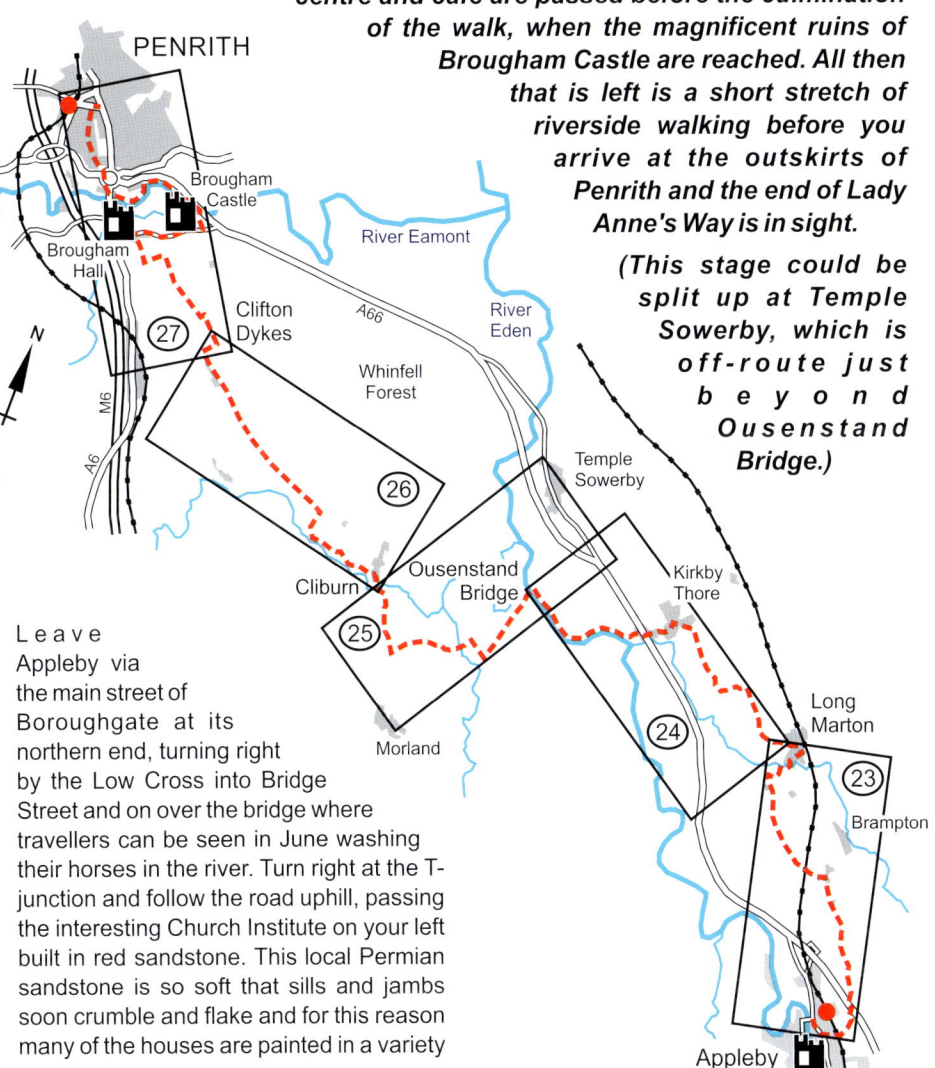

Leave Appleby via the main street of Boroughgate at its northern end, turning right by the Low Cross into Bridge Street and on over the bridge where travellers can be seen in June washing their horses in the river. Turn right at the T-junction and follow the road uphill, passing the interesting Church Institute on your left built in red sandstone. This local Permian sandstone is so soft that sills and jambs soon crumble and flake and for this reason many of the houses are painted in a variety

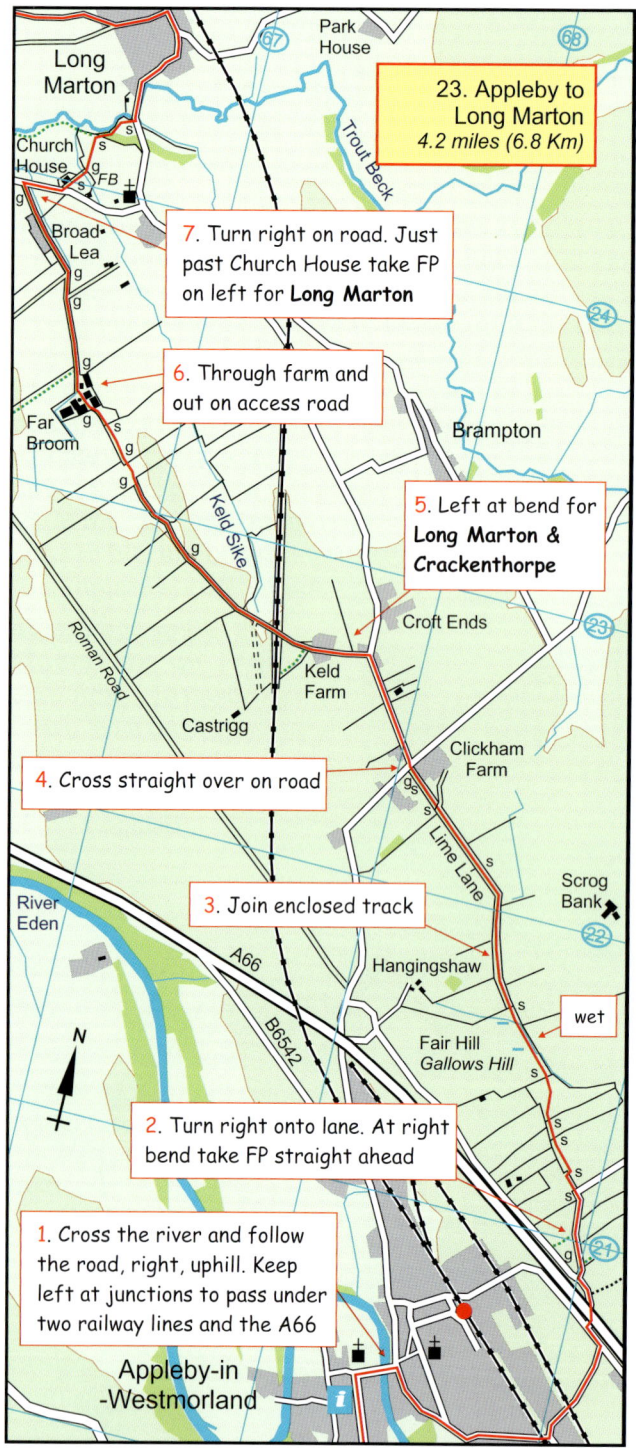

of colours to protect them. Next to the Institute can be seen a wooden door frame built into the red stone at the side of the road, and you may puzzle in vain (as I did) as to what lies beyond.

Take the road off to your left known as Drawbriggs Lane, with a road sign to Hilton and Murton. After passing under a railway line take the road on your left, Garbridge Lane, and soon you will pass under a further railway line.

The once derelict line above you is now being restored by a dedicated team of volunteers. The line originally ran from Penrith, via Appleby to Kikby Stephen, but passenger traffic ceased in 1962. Although only the section of track between Appleby and Warcop remains, it is hoped to reinstate the whole route in the future.

On reaching a T-junction turn left. Follow the road round to the right under the A66 and turn right at the first road, known as Hungriggs Lane but unmarked (GR 690209).

The other road straight ahead is part of the old

Roman road which is one of the routes Lady Anne would have taken out of Appleby, but most of which is now under the A66 and so is of no use to us. The Pikes of Murton and Dufton now come into view with a superb sighting of High Cup Nick in the middle, bringing back memories of the Pennine Way for many. This horse-shoe of vertical crags near the rim of High Cup Nick, known as the Whin Sill, is one of the best examples of its type in all of Britain.

Go through a gate which appears padlocked but isn't, apart from the weeks of Appleby Fair (if this is the case, retrace your steps to the junction and turn right for a few yards to reach a footpath/stile on your right. Follow the path across a corn field and turn left on a road). Carry on along this metalled road, leaving it when it eventually turns to the right to reach a farm, just past a footpath on your right signed to Brampton & Murton. Go over the stile ahead of you beside a gate and carry on in this way through three fields. In the fourth one keep the hedge on your left until it performs a dog leg left, then from here walk diagonally right downhill to go over a stile in the bottom of the field. If there is a crop in the field you may prefer to do as we did and walk round the headland to reach the stile. The next field is formerly Gallows Hill and now Fair Hill. Keep the hedge on your right to reach a further stile.

The field is so named because this is where the travellers gather in the second week in June to commence the business of horse-trading, as mentioned in the previous chapter. The travelling people come from all over the country and can often be seen in the area in the days before the event, camped by the road sides en route to Fair Hill. Apart from the gleaming modern caravans you may see the original horse-drawn versions, many gaily painted in traditional style. Stalls are set up in the field selling a variety of goods, fortunes are told and camp fires are lit in the evenings. The Appleby Horse Fair is a major tourist attraction, with visitors coming from all over the world and the peace and tranquillity of the area is disturbed for a while. But all things come to an end and eventually everything is cleared away and the field resumes its natural life-cycle.

You now enter a wide path which takes you all the way to Clickham Farm. As you approach the farm, leave the track as it swings to the right on its way through the farm buildings. Keep straight ahead over a stile and along a slightly overgrown stretch of green lane. Go through a gate/stile, to pass in front of the farmhouse and out onto the road (GR 680224). Go straight across the road and along the road opposite, signposted to 'Marton, Knock, Milburn'. Where the road curves to the right, take the path on the left signed to 'Long Marton and Crackenthorpe'. Pass Keld Farm and go over the railway bridge - this is the Settle/Carlisle line and you may be fortunate enough to be crossing when one of the steam trains is passing under it. Give it a wave from me as you lean over the parapet - childish I know, but who cares!

This is a good lane, with a hedge either side, and is followed for about half a mile until a metal gate across your path gives access to open fields. Keep the same direction with a small ditch on your left to reach a gate ahead. Follow the fence on your left to reach a further metal gate and stile before dropping down the hill to reach another gate which gives access to Far Broom Farm. Keep your eyes peeled for the directional arrow which guides you to the right of two enormous storage bins and then round to the left of the farmhouse. The route is now obvious all the way to Broad Lea Farm and so out onto the road (GR 663240).

Turn right here and after approximately 100 yards take the path on the left directly after Church House, marked 'Long Marton'. (If wanting to visit Long Marton Church, keep straight on at this point, following the road into Long Marton). Keeping the wall on your left, go over the footbridge and gate at the end of the field and walk diagonally left towards a telegraph pole. Keep the pole to your left and from here a wooden stile may be seen in the fence ahead after which you must drop down diagonally right to the river bank. Turn right, following the river and short-cutting a loop in it, to keep on in the same direction and reach the road. A left turn will take you over the bridge and up to the village of Long Marton.

This is a delightful village, built predominantly of red sandstone and well worth closer scrutiny. There is an amazing mixture of houses of every conceivable date and style, and it even includes a thatched cottage. On the lintel of Mid-Town Farmhouse can be seen an interesting inscription. This was presumably put there by the first couple to inhabit the house in 1740 and has remained a lasting memorial to them: 'John Bellas, Margareef his wife 1740'. The railway station at the far end of the village was closed in 1970. It has been restored over the last fifteen years and is now a holiday let.

The village church is situated approximately half a mile south of the village and is one of the oldest in the county, built in the twelfth century on the site of an earlier wooden structure. Of particular interest are the stone carvings, both outside above the doorways and also inside, one above a window and the other above a doorway.

In the main street you'll see a telephone box on your right, in front of Old Butchers Barn, and a road opposite called Stephens Gate. Turn left here following the road and when it curves right to reach the primary school, two tracks appear ahead either side of a house. Take the one on the right, which is tarmac initially and is your route out of the village (GR 665245). A backward glance along this lane gives a superb view of Great Dun Fell, with the white shape of the radar mast on its summit whilst ahead of you the Lakeland Fells beckon. Follow the tarmac, ignoring all tracks off it, to reach a fork in the track where the tarmac ends. Take the fork to the right, signed to 'Kirkby Thore'.

The track carries on for approximately half a mile before it turns sharp left through a metal gate marked 'Kirkby Thore'. Follow this bridleway as it drops down the field side, passing over Keld Sike and on up to Sleastonhow Farm. Your way lies straight ahead through the farm buildings and out onto the lane. A metal gate opposite is an ideal spot to relax and take in the extensive panorama which now

Door at Long Marton

unfolds: Wild Boar Fell is on your left and the Howgill Fells lie directly ahead with the distant Lakeland hills to the right. A right turn here along the lane will take you all the way to Kirkby Thore.

There are impressive views along here of Cross Fell which, at 2930ft, is the highest of the Pennines. Before leaving the proximity of the Pennines, mention must be made of the notorious 'Helm Wind'. This is a local wind of great force which reaches westwards along the crest of the Pennines from Brough. It rushes over the escarpment towards the valley where it meets a roll of cloud known as the Helm Bar, and it is between these these two points that the wind vents its fury. Crops have been levelled, buildings damaged and people blown over in its wake. As a precaution, houses in the fellside villages are built without north- or east-facing windows. More mundanely, the local gypsum works also features prominently in the landscape hereabouts.

There is just a shop in the village, plus a camp site half a mile outside Kirkby Thore on the A66

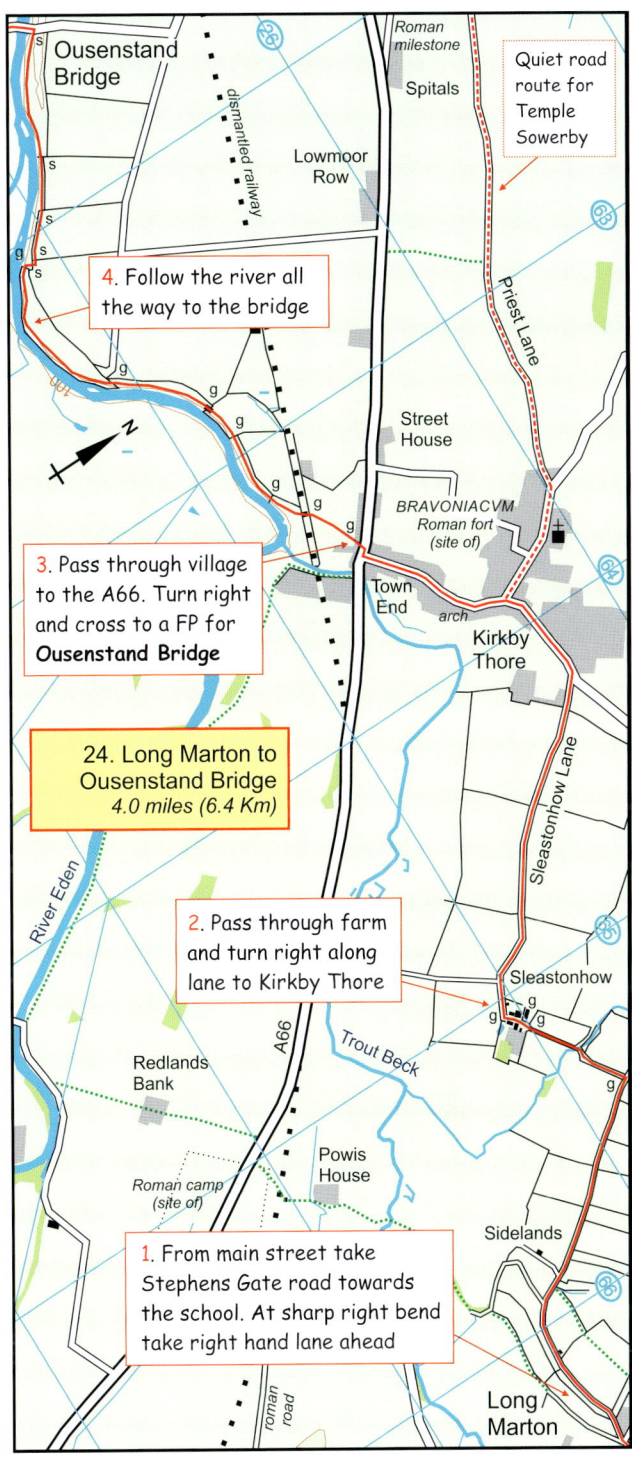

4. Follow the river all the way to the bridge

3. Pass through village to the A66. Turn right and cross to a FP for **Ousenstand Bridge**

24. Long Marton to Ousenstand Bridge
4.0 miles (6.4 Km)

2. Pass through farm and turn right along lane to Kirkby Thore

1. From main street take Stephens Gate road towards the school. At sharp right bend take right hand lane ahead

Approaching Kirkby Thore

in the direction of Penrith. Places of interest in the village include the hall, which is of medieval origin whilst of much earlier date is the site of a Roman Fort, north-west of the main street.

On reaching Kirkby Thore turn left to go through the village to reach the A66, but not before a decision is made.

If you are splitting Stage Six and staying in Temple Sowerby there is a choice of routes. If you don't mind road bashing, there is a route from here along quiet roads, for a distance of 2¼ miles which takes you straight there and is described subsequently. Alternatively follow the main route description to Ousenstand Bridge, from where you need to divert off route for just over a mile to Temple Sowerby, but it is all on footpaths.

TEMPLE SOWERBY ALTERNATIVE BY ROAD

Having turned left to reach the village, go right when you reach Cross Street, which is just before the shop and is signed to Newbiggin. On reaching a fork in the road, with Kirkby Thore Primary School at the junction, take the left fork along Priest Lane, not marked but shown on the OS map. Follow this very quiet road for approximately 1.3 miles and enjoy the stunning views of the Pennines away to your right. (There's even a bench about two-thirds of the way along). The road turns sharp left at SD620267, to reach what was the old A66. Turn right here to reach Temple Sowerby (there is a footpath on the opposite side of the road). The village now has its own by-pass (2007) and so this road is almost traffic free. However it's worth a very short detour left, just beyond the house on the corner, to seek out an old Roman Milestone which stands beside the old road and is surrounded by railings.

Next day, to rejoin the main route at Ousenstand Bridge, leave Temple Sowerby in a south-easterly direction, the same way you came in. When you reach the last house on your right, just before the road off right to Brough & Scotch Corner, go right, directly in front of the house, and signed to the River Eden. Passing right of two properties called Red Brows and Maple Lea, follow the path through a gate and then drop down beneath the A66. Once through the underpass, turn left and follow the path round to reach a stile ahead of you. Go over here with a wall on your left and through a further stile, keep on with the wall on your left to reach another stile in the bottom left corner of the field. Once over this keep on with a wall now on your right to reach a farm track. Turn right here to reach Skygarth Farm. Just before the farmhouse, go left with the waymarks along a track which takes you away from the farm to reach a bridge over a disused railway line. Drop down left here, passing the old railway station (now converted into a house) before eventually reaching the riverbank. Follow this all the way to Ousenstand Bridge. Turn right here to rejoin the main route description.

MAIN ROUTE

At the junction with the A66 turn right and almost immediately you will see a footpath sign on the opposite side of the road, between two houses. Cross this very busy road with great care and take the footpath between the houses, signed to 'Ousenstand Bridge'. Cross the field slightly right, towards the disused railway line - a yellow marker should be visible ahead - and follow the directional arrows over the line, thus avoiding the area underneath the dismantled bridge which looks rather unstable. Keep in the same direction to reach the River Eden. Turn right and follow its banks for approximately 1½ miles. It is a pleasure to get back to riverside pastures after all the farm tracks which preceded this section of the walk. The river here is deep and wide and glides smoothly along, whilst cows and sheep graze the grasslands on either side, creating a typically English pastoral scene.

Follow the riverside path over gates and stiles until at GR 620248 your path diverts briefly from the river, through a gate, where you turn immediately right following a fence right to go over a little plank bridge.

Go over a stile and turn immediately left following a wire fence for the length of one field. At the end of this a further stile takes you back to the riverside once more. Ousenstand Bridge eventually comes into

Ousenstand Bridge

view, built in the mellow red sandstone and making a very pretty picture as it straddles the river.

TEMPLE SOWERBY OPTION BY FOOTPATH

If staying in Temple Sowerby, go straight across the road and follow the riverside footpath ahead, signed to Temple Sowerby & Eden Bridge. Go over an iron step stile at the far end of the field, turn left and follow the edge of the next field to a further stile. This takes you back to the riverbank. Follow the river initially and then head diagonally uphill, aiming for the top side of a stand of trees. Go over a stream and keeping the trees on your left and an old Railway Station (now converted) over to your right, keep straight on. Very soon you need to curve steeply uphill right to reach a gate and a bridge taking you over the disused railway line. Once over here keep straight on towards Skygarth Farm.

As you approach the farm buildings, follow the waymarkers round to the right to shortly come out onto the farm road. Turn right here following the farm road, away from the house. When the road curves away right, go left beside a stone wall to reach a stile ahead. Once over here go uphill with a wall on your right, over two more stiles to reach the tunnel beneath the A66. Go through the underpass and turn right to follow the path uphill to reach a road. Go left here to the centre of Temple Sowerby. You will need to retrace your steps back down to Ousenstand Bridge the following day to rejoin the route.

Temple Sowerby has a pub, The Kings Arms, which has accommodation, restaurant and bar.

The village is a mixture of sixteenth century rubble and thatch buildings intermingled with eighteenth and nineteenth century buildings set around a green. The name is derived from the Knights Templar, a religious and military order, who became lords of the manor in the thirteenth century. Suppressed by Pope Clement V and Philip 1V of France, the estates were subsequently given to the Knights Hospitallers who retained them until the Reformation.

Temple Sowerby

The road through the village is on the line of the Roman Road from York to Brougham and a remnant of this period lies half a mile south east of the village in the form of a Roman Milestone still in its original position. In the late eighteenth century the village lay on the Penrith to Darlington turnpike road and became an important stop-over for travellers. It was a major trading centre with large numbers of livestock passing through on their way to the four annual fairs held in the area.

Temple Sowerby can lay claim to being one of the few Westmorland villages which still retains its maypole and with the advent of the new bypass in 2007 can reclaim its title of 'the Queen of Westmorland Villages'.

MAIN ROUTE

From Ousenstand Bridge turn left on a minor road and follow it for just under a mile to reach a T-junction (GR 611240). Turn right here and after 400 yards you will pass the walled garden of Crossrigg Hall on the left, followed by a bridleway. Turn left here along a good track and, as you pass through the gate, take a

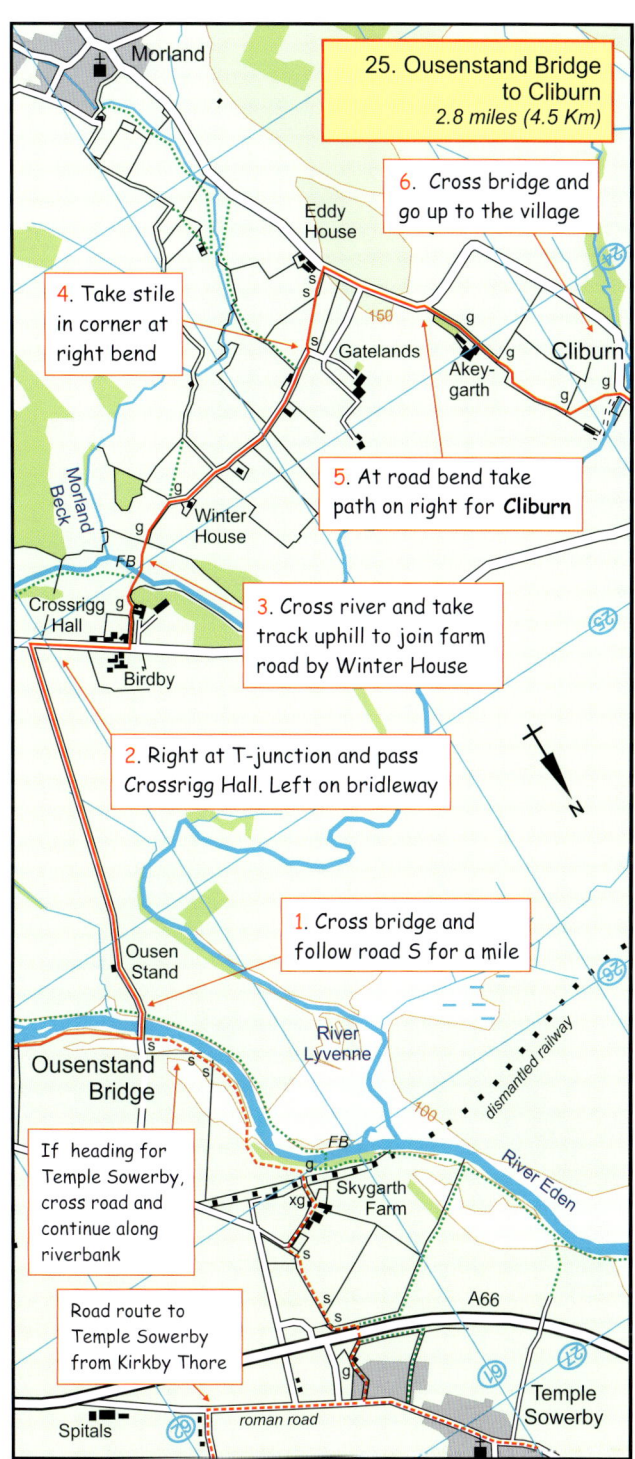

25. Ousenstand Bridge to Cliburn
2.8 miles (4.5 Km)

moment to glance up at an old notice on the barn wall which states, 'The bridge below is closed to all cart & motor traffic', a relic of an earlier age. Also note the Victorian post box below, the last one you saw being at Great Ormside. This lovely track, flanked by beech hedging, leads you out into open fields. In spring, the grounds on your right are carpeted with miniature daffodils which can be glimpsed through the hedge. Drop down to the river, passing a dovecot on your right which helps frame the entrance to an old stable block.

Local legend has it that this area houses a ghost and contains an archway through which no dog will pass. This is all part of Crossrigg Hall estate which was home to Commander Richard Torbock and his younger brother Cornish Torbock until 1994. The hall was built in 1864 to a Jacobean design and was enlarged and remodelled by Joseph Torbock, a wealthy Middlesbrough industrialist in 1915. This Edwardian house remained largely unaltered until the death of the two brothers. Most of the wallpapers, embroidered curtains and fittings were original. Pale oak panelling, polished oak flooring and marble mantelpieces were just some of the fascinating Victorian and Edwardian features. The whole estate was auctioned off in 1994 along with oil paintings and family heirlooms. The hall is now a luxury wedding venue but some of the original features have been kept.

Crossrigg stable block

Cross the River Lyvennet by a bridge with elaborate cast iron railings, although officially the right of way is over the ford to the left of the bridge. Carry on uphill towards a wooden gateway, following the direction of the arrow along the obvious track to reach Winter House. Go through the small gate to the left of the double gate, thus avoiding the private area around the house. Follow the farm lane, ignoring a track off to the left which takes you down to Morland Beck.

Keep on the main track until it turns sharp right (GR 597237). At this juncture go over the stile directly ahead of you, and carry on across the field towards a stile at the fence corner ahead. Once over this, go through the next field, with the fence on your right to reach the road. Turn right here and follow the road until it turns sharp left. Turn right here following the sign to Cliburn.

Follow this farm track to the buildings of Akeygate and go through the metal gate ahead which is to the left of a large building. Keep straight on through a further metal gate and follow the field edge as it does a dog-leg downhill. At the end of this field go through a further gate and bear diagonally left over the brow of a hill to drop down to the River Leith which is spanned by a double arched sandstone bridge. Cliburn and the church of St. Cuthbert can be seen up the hillside ahead as you drop down to the river.

Turn right onto the road, over the bridge and go up the hill to the village. As you enter the main street you will pass the church on your left, hidden behind an avenue of yew trees. It has a Norman chancel arch and two inscribed Roman stones which are set into the porch walls. The church stands in a prominent position above the river Leith, and commands

St. Cuthbert Church, Cliburn

extensive views of the Pennine range of hills.

Your route lies left directly after the church, and goes through the buildings of Rectory Farm. Turn right between the farm buildings (well way-marked), go through the metal gate ahead and bear left through a metal gate on your left. Pass through this concrete area with a tall silage bin on your left and go through another metal gate in the far right hand corner and follow the track down towards the river. Carry straight on as the track bears left to the river, keeping below a steep bank on your right and ignoring the vague track which climbs the hillside. Go through a gate ahead and keep on in the same general direction to pass a sandstone outcrop which could be a useful source of refuge in bad weather.

From here the official path follows the green track, which carries on upwards towards Leith House, before dropping down to rejoin your original line of travel, beneath a bank of scrub. Keep on to pass a lonely stone gatepost. Go over the stile at the hedge corner ahead and carry on with the hedge on your right, to reach a little wooden bridge beside an old stile. Cross this bridge and bear slightly left to reach a stile beside the river. Once over here follow a path all the way to Commonholme Bridge.

Turn right at the road and follow this for about 300 yards to the T-junction (GR 576253) and then turn left. This is the start of just under two miles of unavoidable road walking. Fortunately there is plenty of grass verge, which is infinitely preferable to sharing the tarmac with the traffic, some of which can be travelling fast on this straight stretch.

Whinfell Forest, which is your companion on the right, would have been very familiar to Lady Anne as she travelled through it on her way from Brougham Castle to Appleby. At its north western boundary lies Julian's Bower which was once a shooting lodge built by Roger Clifford in the fourteenth century for his mistress. Legend has it that during a hunt led by Robert de Clifford, a stag died whilst leaping over a hedge, followed by a hound known as Hercules, which also died of exhaustion. The chase had been long and hard and to commemorate the courage of the animals the stag's horns were nailed to a nearby oak.

Records show that there was in fact an oak tree in 1633 on which the horns of a stag were nailed. These became embedded in the growing wood and were almost overgrown. Vandals broke off one horn and then the other, and Lady Anne herself remarked in her diaries of her sadness that no horns

Sandstone outcrop near Cliburn

remained and that the tree was almost dead. Part of the tree existed up till 1790 and its roots remained until 1807. Lord Hothfield had part of the root on his writing desk as a memento at least until 1967. Nothing is now left of the hunting lodge but a farm exists on the spot and is known as Julian's Bower.

Keep straight on, passing through the hamlet of Clifton Dykes. Immediately before the last house on your right, you reach a track on your right (GR 547270). Follow this farm track to Highground Farm.

Before reaching the farm buildings, at the end of the first field, you will reach a metal gate either side of the farm track. Go through the left one (the path is not obvious on the ground) and keep the hedge on your right to reach a stile at the end of the field. Once over this, go through a gate and carry on with a fence on your left to eventually reach the road. Penrith can now be seen ahead with Beacon Hill rising behind it, topped by its eighteenth century sandstone tower. The beacon was used at the time of the border raids, when the embers were hardly ever cold.

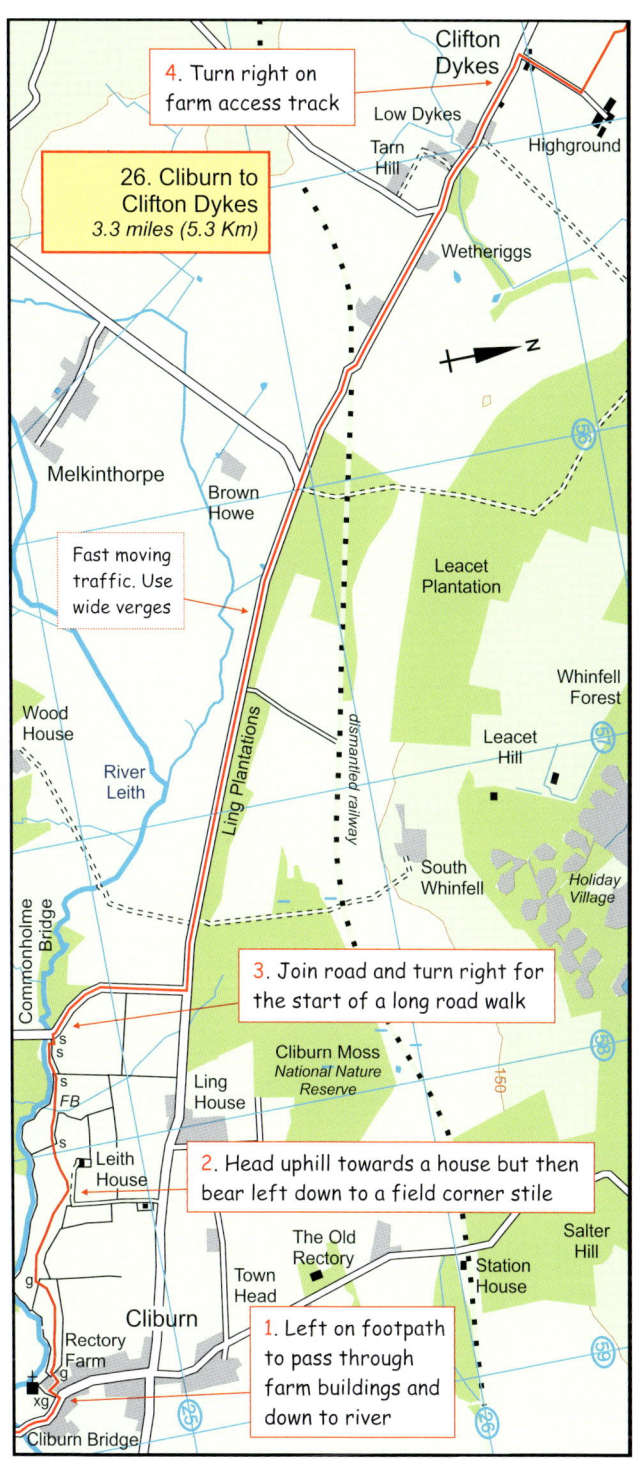

26. Cliburn to Clifton Dykes
3.3 miles (5.3 Km)

1. Left on footpath to pass through farm buildings and down to river
2. Head uphill towards a house but then bear left down to a field corner stile
3. Join road and turn right for the start of a long road walk
4. Turn right on farm access track

Fast moving traffic. Use wide verges

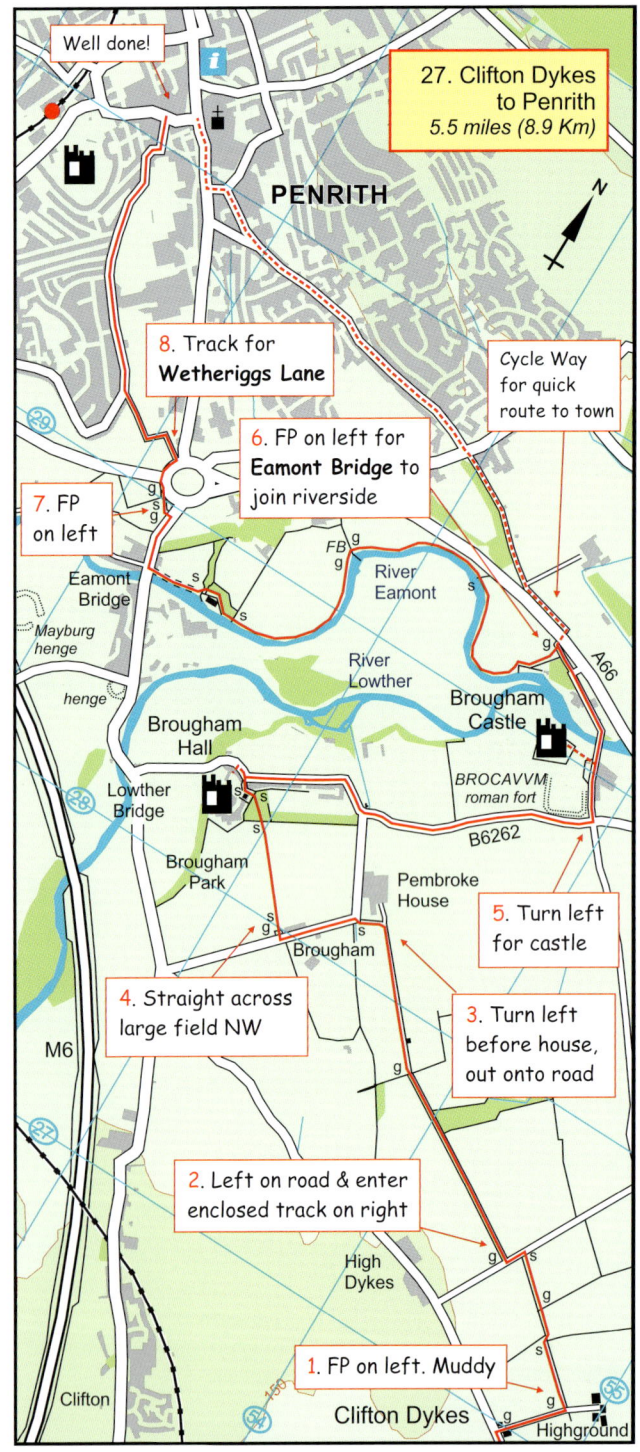

Turn left on the road and after a few yards, at the end of the field on your right, is an opening, and a section of broken down wall. Turn right here, through a waymarked gate, and follow this lovely green lane, which is lined with ancient hedging to reach a gate. Once through the gate, take the track straight ahead towards Pembroke House. As you reach the gateway to the back of the house, turn left in front of the stone wall and follow it down to the road (GR 534282).

Turn left at the road and when you reach a group of cottages on the right, after approximately 200 yards, go right here through a gate beside Keepers Cottage. Go through a tiny field and a waymarked gate to reach a very large field. Go straight across here towards a broadleaved plantation, and a stile, which is approximately 100 yards to the right of some house roofs. Go over the stile and enter the plantation, where you need to walk diagonally left through the trees to reach the road. (The last few yards are over a stile and across the corner of a garden).

Turn left on the road and follow it round to the

right to arrive at Brougham Hall.

The impressive gateway which greets you frames studded oak doors and incorporates a smaller door through which you enter, known as a postern gate. Rumour has it that the door came from Brougham Castle just a mile away, probably 'rescued' after Lady Anne's death when the castle fell into disrepair.

The ruins of Brougham Hall are undergoing restoration and there are exciting plans for its future. At present, the stables and carriage houses are occupied by local craftspeople selling their wares, and there are plans for a museum and library, amongst other projects. Of more pressing interest may be the cafe which is situated in this block.

The hall's history is very chequered, but there was certainly a hall on this site at the time of the Norman Conquest held by the de Veteriponts of Brougham Castle and ancestors of Lady Anne. She herself bought the freehold of the hall in 1651 for £1,500. During the medieval period members of the de Veteriponts wished to enlarge their hunting grounds around Whinfell Forest, but there was an obstacle in the guise of the village of Ninekirks. In those days nothing stood in the way of the Lord of the Manor, and so Ninekirks was demolished and the villagers were forced to move and resettle close to Brougham Hall. The villagers were now three miles away from their own parish church of Ninekirks, which had been spared, and so a chapel was built close by to administer the sacraments, except for burial; it also acted as the village school for a period.

The chapel can be visited but the key must be obtained first from one of the craft shops. This is yet another building that Lady Anne resurrected from ruin in 1659, and a year later she did the same for the church of Ninekirks. From the exterior, the buildings have many similarities; however, Brougham Chapel was completely altered at the beginning of the eighteenth century, and nothing of Lady Anne's work remains. Even her inscription under her arms in the east end has disappeared. Fortunately, this is not the case at Ninekirks, where little has changed in the intervening years.

Brougham Hall reached its heyday in the nineteenth century, when it was altered beyond recognition to become a place fit for the Lord Chancellor of England to live in, this being Chancellor Brougham - the same who gave his name to the Brougham carriage. The hall became known as the 'Windsor of the North', and must have been an impressive sight with its oak panelled rooms and antique furniture.

An incredible door knocker nearly two feet across can be seen on a door in the outer

wall, close by the chapel. The original was made as a replica of the Durham Cathedral Sanctuary Knocker, and represents a devil's head with a radiating mane. This was made hollow, and legend has it that a light used to shine out through the eyes and mouth, creating an eerie sight on a dark winter's night. The present knocker is a copy of the original, which disappeared from the hall in the 1960's.

Leave the hall from your place of entry and take the road straight ahead along the B6262, down the hill towards Brougham Castle. Follow this quiet road as it curves to the right and then left, following the signs to Appleby, Penrith and Brougham Castle. When you reach a very high stone wall on the left, a peep over here will give you superb views of the castle which stands in splendid isolation with nothing around to detract from its beauty. At the cross roads (GR 539289) a left turn will bring you to the castle entrance, where for a small sum, you can gain admittance.

About half a mile away from this junction, on the A66 towards Appleby, stands the Countess' Pillar, erected in 1656 by Lady Anne to commemorate her last parting with her mother. She also left an annuity of four pounds to be given annually to the poor of the parish of Brougham. This tradition is still re-enacted each year by the rector of Brougham Parish, on the stone table next to the pillar known as the Dolestone.

A further 1½ miles away to the north of the A66 (GR 559300) lies Ninekirks church which was mentioned earlier. Services are seldom held there, apart from Evensong once a month during the summer, but the church is looked after and is a place of pilgrimage to many. The horse-box pews are still there as well as the Rood Screen and the three-decker pulpit, all built in 1660 to Lady Anne's specifications. Her final touch was a cartouche on the east wall with the initials AP and 1660 on it. The church stands in isolation in the middle of a field, bordered on one side by the River Eamont and backed by the Pennine hills.

Brougham Castle is an extensive ruin, the oldest part of which is the thirteenth century keep, built by one of Lady Anne's ancestors, Robert de Vipont. Subsequent ancestors added to this defensive complex, which commanded an impregnable position beside the River Eamont. A garrison was stationed at the castle which gives an idea of the importance of its position in the Eden Valley. Certainly the Romans thought so, as they built a fort here to guard the river crossing. South - east of the castle lie the remains of the fort known as Brocavum which housed at least 1000 troops. The site is on private property, but some of the inscribed stones which were unearthed are on display at the castle.

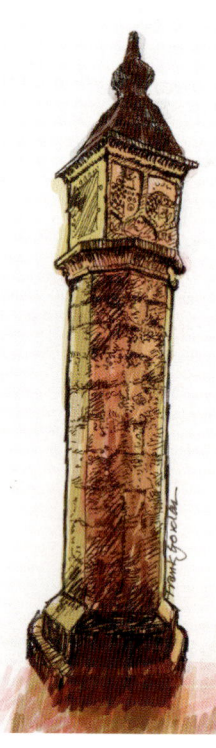

The castle was still in use at the beginning of the seventeenth century, and records show that both James I and Charles I stayed there during this period. However, when Lady Anne visited Brougham after the Civil War she found it in a very ruinous state. She started restoring it to its former glory in 1651, and on completion her diaries tell us that she spent five months there "and I had not layne in this Brougham Castle in Thirty Seaven years till now".

As always there was a stone bearing an inscription recording the repair works, put in place by Lady Anne. This is now on display in the entrance building.

THE BROVHAM CASTLE WAS REPAIRED BY THE LADIE ANNE CLIFFORD COVNTESSE DOWAGER OF PEMBROOKE, DORSETT AND MONTGOMERY, BARONESSE CLIFFORD WESTMERLAND AND VESEIE, LADIE OF THE HONOVR OF SKIPTON IN CRAVEN AND HIGH

SHERIFFESSE BY INHERITANCE, OF THE COVNTIE OF WESTMERLAND, IN THE YEARES 1651 AND 1652 AFTER IT HAD LAYEN ROVINOVS EVER SINCE ABOVT AVGVST 1617 WHEN KING IAMES LAY IN IT FOR A TIME IN HIS IOVRNIE OVT OF SKOTLAND TOWARDS LONDON VNTIL THIS TIME.

ISA. CHAP. 58 VERSE 12. GODS NAME BE PRAISED

The stone above the outer gatehouse which bears the inscription "thys made Roger" probably refers to the 5th baron. This stone was found nearby in the river and was positioned above the gatehouse in the nineteenth century, approximately where Lady Anne's inscription would have been.

Brougham was possibly Lady Anne's favourite castle, for it was here that her father was born and where her mother died. She spent a great deal of time here, and it is perhaps fitting that she should end her days in this idyllic spot by the river. Few women can have made such an impression on so many people during their lifetime, and be still held with such regard over 300 years later.

Journeys were a way of life to Lady Anne as she travelled between her castles with her retinue of servants and followers, and we can only marvel at her tenacity when faced with yet another trek along those perilous roads. Her family tried to persuade her to take life more easily in later years, but her retort was that she may as well die in her horse-litter as in her bed!

Lady Anne died in the state bed chamber at Brougham Castle on Wednesday 22nd March 1676, after enduring great pain, her last words being "I thank God I am very well". A great procession followed her body, which was encased in lead and taken by coach past the Countess' Pillar on her last journey to St. Lawrence's Church in Appleby.

Brougham Castle

Your own journey is also almost at an end, but there is still a short way to go. After visiting the castle and your last link with Lady Anne, carry on along the road over the bridge, where in springtime the buttresses are covered with aubretia in bloom. Follow this road and when it curves right to meet the A66, fork left and join what used to be the old road, to reach a footpath sign on the left to 'Eamont Bridge' (GR 535293).

Decisions need to be made here. The main route follows the riverside path for 1½ miles towards Eamont Bridge before the final mile north west into Penrith. However if time is short and you don't mind the tarmac, the shortest way from here is beneath an underpass on your right, signed Penrith, which also coincides with Cycle Track No. 71 and is a distance of 1½ miles. (Follow the track beneath the A66 which becomes a road with accompanying footpath. Eventually you reach a crossroads and the Cross Keys Inn. Go straight over the road and along the road ahead named Carleton Road/Winters Park which takes you all the way into Penrith).

MAIN ROUTE

Follow the 'Eamont Bridge' sign across the field to the riverbank, where the remains of a diving board and paddling pool will be seen. In the 1960's these were used by the schoolchildren of Penrith for their swimming lessons. Turn right and follow the river upstream for approximately 1½ miles towards Eamont Bridge. Eventually you reach the abuttments of a derelict suspension bridge, as you approach a copse of trees. Go over a stile here to enter the wood. Follow the main track through the trees, until it curves left to reach a further stile. Go over here and turn right onto a track which leads you onto the road at Eamont Bridge.

Cross over the road and turn right, heading

Window, Eamont Bridge

towards a large roundabout. Directly before this on the left you will find a footpath. Go through a gate here and follow the wall on your right as it turns right, to reach a further stile ahead and so out onto the A66. Go left a few yards to cross this busy junction - the noise and speed of the traffic can come as a great shock after the peace and tranquillity of your riverside walking. Turn right on the opposite side of the road, until you reach a tarmac path on your left. Follow this path until it comes out onto Wetheriggs Lane. A right turn here will lead you eventually past Ullswater Community College. After passing Sainsburys follow the road as it curves round to the right to reach the centre of Penrith.

There is plenty of accommodation in the town, and a caravan site which allows tents if space is available.

Penrith was once the capital of Cumbria and is close to the M6 motorway, giving easy access to London and Glasgow. It marks a gateway to the Lake District and the North Pennines and is a very popular shopping centre, being famed for its toffee and fudge and, of course, the traditional Cumberland sausage. There is little left of the Permian sandstone castle from which the town gets its name of Penrhudd, the red hill. Close by in St. Andrew's churchyard is said to be buried the giant Ewan Caesarius, a hero of great strength who ruled Cumbria in Saxon times. The arrangement of four hog-back stones and an ancient cross are known as the Giant's Grave, and have become a great tourist attraction. There is much of architectural interest in Penrith and the many yards linking the main thoroughfares are worthy of some exploration. William and Dorothy Wordsworth attended school in the town and this building can still be seen facing onto St. Andrew's churchyard.

In the centre of the town is the market square, with a monument and clocktower as its focal point. This was built in 1861 to commemorate the death of Philip Musgrave of Eden Hall, cousin to Lady Anne, and makes a fitting end to your journey.

Congratulations! You have completed Lady Anne's Way and are now free to celebrate in your own chosen fashion. There is certainly no shortage of pubs and other places of refreshment in the town.

Anyone with time to spare may care to savour the delights of the Lake District by continuing to Pooley Bridge on Ullswater which is only about five miles away; from there, a host of delightful walking opportunities present themselves. An alternative would be to make your way to Carlisle via part of the Eden Way, and then start the Cumbria Way which passes through the centre of the Lake District and finishes at Ulverston some 75 miles away. The choice is yours.

Penrith

A SOUVENIR OF LADY ANNE'S WAY

A woven badge is available from the author, either telephone: 01729 824638 or email: sheilamgordon@googlemail.com

Further information is available from the website:
www.ladyannesway.co.uk

SELECT BIBLIOGRAPHY

BOUCH C.M.L. - **The Lady Anne** (*The Print Shop, Appleby 1954*)

CLIFFORD D.J.H. - **The Diaries of Lady Anne Clifford** (*Alan Sutton Publishing Ltd 1990*)

EMMET C. - **The Eden Way** (*Cicerone Press 1990*)

EYRES P. - **Lady Anne's Way** (*New Arcadian Press c.1987*)

HAMILTON J. - **Mallerstang Dale** (*Broadcast Books 1993*)

HANSON N. - **Walking Through Eden** (*Futura Publications 1991*)

HOLMES M. - **Proud Northern Lady** (*Phillmore and Co., Chichester 1973*)

MITCHELL W.R. - **High Dale Country** (*Souvenir Press Ltd 1991*)

PONTEFRACT E. & HARTLEY M. - **Wensleydale** (*Smith Settle Ltd 1988*)

PONTEFRACT E. & HARTLEY M. - **Wharfedale** (*J.M.Dent & Sons, London 1938*)

RAISTRICK A. - **The Pennine Dales** (*Arrow Books Ltd 1972*)

ROBERTSON D. & KORONKA P. - **Secrets & Legends of Old Westmorland** (*Pagan Press 1992*)

TYLER DAWN. - **A History of Brougham Hall** (*Ross Features Int. 1988*)

WALKER STEPHEN.- **Nine Standards** (*Hayloft 2008*)

WILLIAMSON G.C. - **Lady Anne Clifford** (*Titus Wilson, Kendall 1922*)

In addition, various local pamphlets and tourist guides, in particular those published by East Cumbria Countryside Project.

Acknowledgements

Thank you, as ever, to Frank for his brilliant drawings and also for his continual support along the way and to my son Russell for all his hard work designing the website. Special thanks to Helen and Pat who both walked many miles of the route with me over the years and who are both sadly no longer with us.

Many thanks to Tony for creating and checking the maps and the route details and also to the Rights of Way officers for the Yorkshire Dales National Park, North Yorkshire Council and Westmorland & Furness Council.

Finally thanks to anyone else who has helped me in any way with this new edition of Lady Anne's Way.

Photos pages 80, 82, 84 & 85 © Frank and Sheila Gordon.

All other photos © Skyware Ltd (unless otherwise stated).

PHOTOS & IMAGES: Front cover - Approaching Brough Castle;

Back cover - (anticlockwise from top right) Knocker, Brougham Hall; Brough Castle; Hawes (Frank Gordon); River Wharfe; Crossing Halton Edge.

Title page illustration - Approaching Buckden (Frank Gordon).

Engraving on page 48 reproduced from a post at the foot of The Highway, Mallerstang.

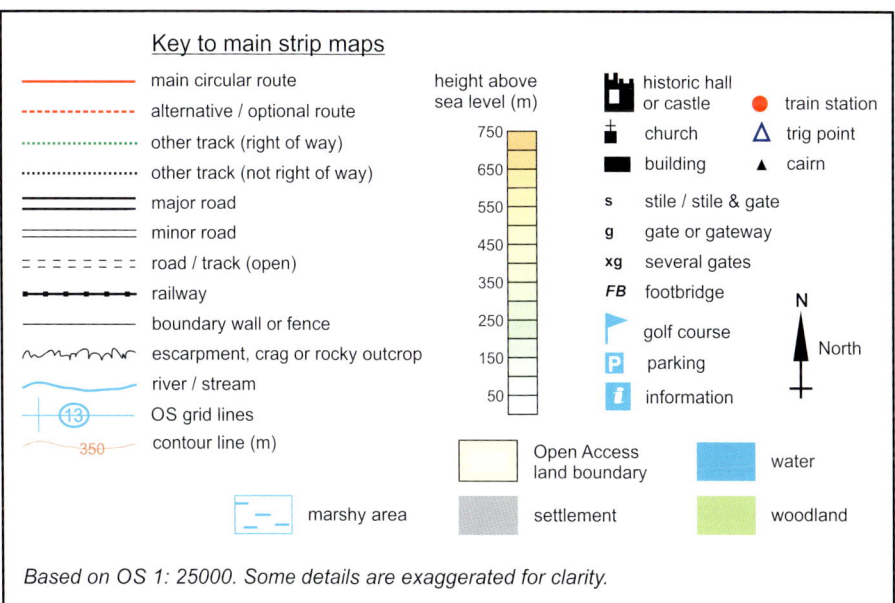

Unique guides to Long Distance walks from Skyware Press:

A Dales High Way

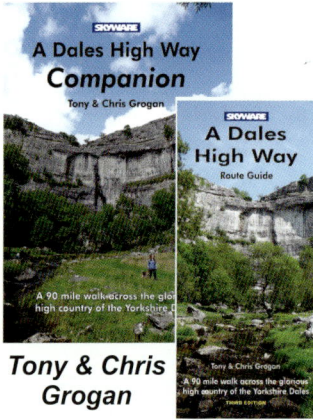

The original guides to a 90 mile walk across the glorious high country of the Yorkshire Dales.

"Promoted through a superbly illustrated Companion book, rich in local geology, history and wildlife, with detailed OS-based maps in an excellent Route Guide, the Dales High Way is a sure-fire winner for all keen Dales walkers,"

- Colin Speakman, Yorkshire Dales Review

A Dales High Way: Route Guide
A Dales High Way Companion

Tony & Chris Grogan

Dales Way

Colin Speakman

The original classic 80 mile trail from Ilkley to Bowness-on-Windermere.

Dales Rail Trails

Tony & Chris Grogan

32 day walks from stations along the fabulous Settle-Carlisle railway.

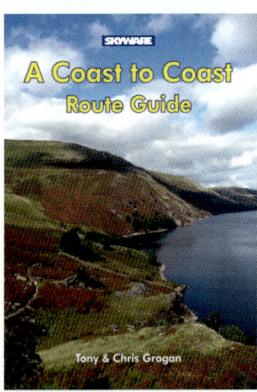

A Coast to Coast Route Guide

Tony & Chris Grogan

Wainwright's classic walk across northern England.

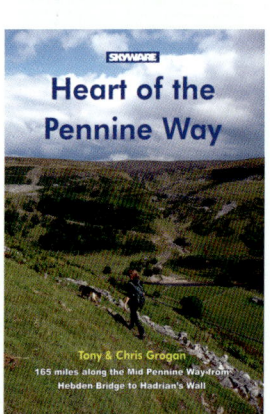

Heart of the Pennine Way

Tony & Chris Grogan

165 miles along the Heart of Britain's premier National Trail.

buy online:
www.skyware.co.uk